LOVE DECLARED

Essays on the Myths of Love

BY DENIS DE ROUGEMONT

Les Personnes du Drame
The Devil's Share
Love in the Western World

Denis de Rougemont

LOVE DECLARED

ESSAYS ON
THE MYTHS OF LOVE

TRANSLATED FROM THE FRENCH

BY *Richard Howard*

BEACON PRESS   BOSTON

PREFATORY NOTE

THIS WORK resumes the argument of several others in which I have spoken of the passion of love, the myths of the soul, and the mystery of the person; [1] it extends their views toward a point from which the eye can gain a more unified perspective of the human phenomenon: body-soul-mind.

Hence these pages will be found to contain new reflections on the *erotic myths* in Western culture, and on the *imaginary characters* of the novel and the opera in whom these myths are exemplified; then a series of observations (in the clinical sense of the word) on *real persons*, whose life stories seem to have been adapted to the dynamic formulas of Don Juan and Tristan; lastly, we return to the chief problem, that of the *person* as defined or denied by the major religions. For any idea of man is an idea of love.

This order may seem surprising. Logical transitions inserted ex post facto between the various chapters of the collection would be little more than a contrivance—and I forswear them in favor of a long Introduction—to vouch for the book's unity and to make acceptable its true subject: that oscillation between the religious and the erotic which is one of the conclusive secrets of the Western psyche.

[1] I refer to *Love in the Western World* (French editions 1939 and 1954), *Doctrine Fabuleuse* (1946), and *Les Personnes du Drame* (1945) in particular.

I see no area, in fact, where inveterate misunderstandings and impatient prejudices keep so many, whether believers or not, from confronting their real problems or from even permitting them to be observed. Freud has revealed some of the motives for such resistance to lucidity; he located them in the conflict between the sexual life and social morality. Before him, Marx had ventured a no less "shocking" analysis of the refusal to face economic realities, in conflict with the ideal of the Victorian bourgeoisie. Both, moreover, remained tributaries of that same Western society whose "good motives" for blinding itself in two vital, well-defined areas they "exposed" with such genius. But these areas (precisely those made taboo by the ruling classes of their day) do not encompass all reality, either of Western man or of man in general. In spite of everything, Marx and Freud shared with the society they attacked a system of thought and certain prejudices which were in their turn to blind them to another order of realities.

I have therefore attempted to reassert the dialectic of *love* and of the *person*, which are the two realities that these great men were obliged by their closed systems to eliminate or suppress.

I have proceeded here on the basis of an inquiry and not of literature, despite the many examples I have chosen among the great authors of the nineteenth and twentieth centuries and quoted as so many facts. What must be found or invented are not objects of language (as one expects of poetry) or of values (as one expects of philosophers), but a truer vision, modifying the subject.

It is not surprising that such an inquiry has more than once taken me far beyond the conclusions of *Love in the Western World*. Some may reproach me for inconsistency. However, if the reader closely considers what follows, he will see that my original theses are not so much negated as corrected. Some arguments have lost their point once they were better oriented within a view of Love which, I shall not be disconcerted to learn, is monistic: the only monism that does not contradict the reality of the person is precisely that of Love, for the very being of Love—its existence, its power, and its essence—ceaselessly recreates the nonillusory multiplicity of persons, and preserves it at the heart of Unity, in order to love it and to be loved by it. That is the entire philosophy I deduce from my essays upon rereading them, though it is here presented only in images and symbols.

CONTENTS

INTRODUCTION
EROTICISM AND THE MYTHS
OF THE SOUL

I

LOVE AND THE PERSON

IN THE CHRISTIANIZED WORLD

Eros, who was a god for the Ancients, is a problem for the Moderns. The god was winged, charming, and secondary; the problem is serious, complex, and cumbersome. But this applies only in the West, for *nothing of the kind is observed in India, in China, or in Africa.* How can we explain this fact? And why has eroticism become an age-old synonym for perversity not only in the legal jargon of the secular State, but in the eyes of sincere and high-principled Christians? To understand the problematic situation of our time, we must look back to the origins of Christianity.

Christian puritanism is a little older than the Gospels: it first appears in the Epistles of Saint Paul. And if it is remarkable that the Gospels, written down soon afterwards, reveal almost no traces of it, we know nonetheless that they were read for centuries in the light of the Pauline polemic against the Gnostics. Now it is the Gnostics who first tried to make the transition from Eros to the Spirit, preferably by extreme means, varying from castration to sacred prostitution, or from the *communio spermatica* of certain Basilidian sects to the general cult of a *sophia aeterna*, an Eternal Feminine exalted far above the biblical creator Jahve. Ceaselessly attacked in their

3

doctrines by the Fathers of the early Church, rigorously persecuted later on by established Christendom, they are the true ancestors of the traditions spread by the Catharist heresy and the Northern mystics (or at least by their vocabulary) from which proceed—by what devious routes we have studied elsewhere—modern lyricism and the novel, which speak of virtually nothing but a "profane" love, without any longer knowing its origin or its goal.[1] The intransigent hostility that opposes the champions of morality to the erotic writers prolongs, though neither camp knows it, a dispute twenty centuries old, but whose terms have been corrupted as all awareness was lost of the spiritual orientations they originally signified.

Let us therefore reconsider these fundamental terms and see if they really permit us to explain why it is in Europe, *and only there*, that religious morality and eroticism have reached this state of permanent conflict, of reciprocal contempt, of rigorous mutual exclusion. No such situation prevails in India, we repeat, nor more generally in the cultures which Christianity has not affected or affected only slightly.

I. CHRISTIANITY IS THE RELIGION OF LOVE. A religion of a God whom the Old Testament defined as the original Being, the creator of the world and the savior of Israel, but whom the New Testament reveals at the *heart* of all men, and in a radically new way: "God is love," Saint John repeats. A religion created by an act of love:

[1] Cf. *Love in the Western World*, rev. ed. (1954), Book II.

4

"God so loved the world that he gave his only begotten Son . . ." A religion whose entire law is summed up by Jesus Christ himself, in a single and unique commandment: "Thou shalt love the Lord thy God, and thy neighbour as thyself." [2] A religion which puts love first among all the virtues: "And now abideth faith, hope, love, these three; but the greatest of these is love." And he who has not love is "become as sounding brass or a tinkling cymbal"; is nothing, in spiritual truth.

2. BECAUSE IT IS A RELIGION OF LOVE, CHRISTIANITY IMPLIES AND POSTULATES THE REALITY OF THE PERSON. The relations which it defines between man and his God are personal. God is personal. The Trinity is composed of three Persons. The model of every human person is given by the Incarnation of Christ son of God in Jesus son of Mary—Jesus Christ being both "true God and true man" according to the Credo. Hence it follows directly that every man converted, recreated by divine love, will become, in the imitation of Jesus Christ, true vocation and true individual, that is: a person distinct but at the same time related by what distinguishes him.

[2] Here are the three convergent texts of the Old and New Testaments:

"Thou shalt love thy neighbour as thyself." Leviticus 19:18.

"Thou shalt love the Lord thy God with all thine heart, and with all thy soul, and with all thy might." Deuteronomy 6:5.

"One of them, which was a lawyer, asked him a question, tempting him, and saying, Master, which is the great commandment in the law? Jesus said unto him, Thou shalt love the Lord thy God with all thy heart, and with all thy soul, and with all thy mind. This is the first and great commandment. And the second is like unto it, Thou shalt love thy neighbour as thyself. On these two commandments hang all the law and the prophets." Matthew 22:35-40.

For to love, one must be distinct from the object of love with which one desires to be united. And for man to be able to love God and first of all to be loved by Him, God must be personal and must be "altogether other" than man. And lastly, for man to be able to love himself, there must be a duality in him between the natural man and the new man recreated by the summons he receives from love. This summons is his vocation, the new life of his person. This life remains in part mysterious, being "hidden with Christ in God," but it manifests itself by acts, in the love of one's neighbor as of oneself. Thus love both distinguishes and relates. It relates to the divine mystery, but also to the mystery of that visible "neighbor" whose person remains invisible.

3. THIS RELIGION OF TOTAL LOVE (LOVE OF GOD, OF ONESELF, AND OF ONE'S NEIGHBOR) HAS NO SACRED BOOKS OF LOVE. In that infinitely varied amalgam of phenomena which only Europe has designated by the single term of love,[3] let us consider the extreme bands of the

---

[3] In Greek "the word *philia* designates any feeling of attachment and affection between two persons, but the philosophers distinguished four kinds: the natural or parental *philia* (*physikè*), uniting those of the same blood; the *philia* between host and guests (*xenikè*), which indicates the importance of the virtues of hospitality; the *philia* between friends (*hetairike*), which alone corresponds to friendship, strictly speaking; lastly, the amorous *philia* (*erotikè*), between persons of the same sex or of different sex. Further, to distinguish the various nuances of love, the Greeks possessed many words, aside from *philia* and *eros*: *eunoia*, designating dedicated devotion; *agapè*, disinterested affection; *storgè*, tenderness; *pothos*, desire; *charis*, gratitude and kindness; *mania*, unleashed passion. This enumeration, moreover, is far from complete. The word *agapè*, quite rare in the pagan texts, was to enjoy a great future, for the first Christians and the Greek-speaking Fathers used it to designate the divine love and the

spectrum: the ultraviolet of the spiritual and the infra-red of the sexual. Our mysticism, the science of divine love, has developed very belatedly, in forms and along paths almost always suspect in the eyes of the ortho-dox.[4] Our sexual ethic has been reduced, over a long period, to a few elementary prohibitions such as may be found in virtually all constituted societies. In spite of treatises by certain Fathers of the Church (prohibiting this or that sexual position because it was contrary to fecundation) and huge tomes of casuistry mostly written in the sixteenth and seventeenth centuries by monks for the use of father confessors, we find no single Christian

brotherly love that prevailed in the 'agapes.' They suspected the word *eros*, and with reason." (Robert Flacelière, *L'Amour en Grèce* [Paris, 1960].) Empedocles designates love by the words *philotès* (analo-gous to *philia*) or *harmonia*. Socrates declared that he possessed only one knowledge, that of *erotikè*. Lastly, the Greeks very clearly dis-tinguished *Aphrodite* (from *aphros*, foam, or sperm of the mutilated god), who presides over physical love, and *Eros*, who governs amo-rous feeling.

It may be objected that our modern languages also possess such words as friendship, tenderness, desire, passion, compassion, charity, etc. Nonetheless they call them all *love*, merely varying the adjec-tives. *And it is precisely this one term which is lacking in Greek, as in every Asian language without exception.* It is characteristic of Christian Europe and of the West as a whole that here alone all the forms of human inclination can be covered by a single vocable, desig-nating not some common substance, but a creative impulse of being which manifests itself in them all. It is inevitable that certain critics will reproach me for "confusing" in these pages divine love, passion, and desire, *agapè, eros,* and *aphros;* but this apparent solecism of vocabulary is the reality of our entire Western culture.

[4] The major phase of Christian mysticism, though predicted by Augustine, was actually constituted and developed only between the twelfth and sixteenth centuries, that is, during the third quarter of the Christian era, and always apart from theology, which has con-tinued to hold it in suspicion: I refer to the final conclusions of Meister Eckhart, of the Admirable Ruysbrœk, of Saint John of the Cross, all condemned by ecclesiastical authority.

equivalent—existing or imaginable—of the *Kama Sutra*, of the Tantras, of so many other treatises on eroticism in the Vedas and the Upanishads, relating the sexual to the divine; still less, of the famous sculptures on the façades of the great Hindu temples, illustrating in the most precise manner the unions of the gods and their wives, for didactic and religious purposes. No secret methods nor sexual magic, no physiology of the mystic pilgrimage, such as the one which the treatises of the Hatha Yoga describe without variation in a thousand years. Nor is there a trace, in Christianity, of those initiation ceremonies, common to most other religions, in which relations between the sexes play a decisive, scrupulously prescribed role. Thus the Africans and the American Indians, the aborigines of Australia yesterday and of the Amazon today, and even the primitives of Polynesia, whose customs are so gentle, all perform rites each more cruel than the next, in order to make the occurrence of puberty sacred and social. Confronted with this same endocrine crisis, Christianity is content with extremely severe moral counsel and vague or aberrant hygienic advice. On one side, rite and physical cruelties which regulate everything; on the other, problems and moral torment.

The Christian churches have always had more success in their efforts to repress and "contain" the sexual instinct than in their attempts (rare, peripheral, indeed heretical) to cultivate and regulate eroticism for spiritual purposes, even within the bounds of marriage. This is because the theologians feared that Eros might be re-

8

garded as divinizing without grace and leading to revelation. "If ye live after the flesh ye shall die," Saint Paul declares. And it was a short step to reduce to the sexual the meaning of "flesh," which, for the Apostle, designated the whole of man (body, soul, intellect) in its natural and fallen reality. In the virgin birth of Jesus, tradition and the faithful alike saw the absence of sex, hence of sin, rather than the positive sign of a divine filiation.[5]

On the other hand, the Christian churches, followed down to our own day by the secular powers, have developed since the first apostolic generation a quite specific *doctrine of marriage* which Gnosticism, significantly, ignores. It is based on several verses of the Epistles and the Gospels which together define a coherent ethic of a personalist nature, and no longer social or sacred as in the other religions. It is only the more striking to note how greatly the spiritual motivations of marriage differ and even contradict each other in Saint Paul. Sometimes he establishes a kind of mystical analogy between the love of the sexes in marriage and the love of Jesus for the community of the faithful: "Husbands, love your wives, even as Christ also loved the church." Sometimes, and more often, he reduces marriage to no more than a concession to nature, a discipline against incontinence: "It is good for a man not to touch a woman. Nevertheless,

[5] The dogma of the Immaculate Conception of the Virgin (1871) isolates and emphasizes this negative element, since there cannot here be a question of a divine filiation of Mary—of an Incarnation other than that of Christ—or else the doctrine would be accepting the tenets of Gnosticism.

to avoid fornication, let every man have his own wife, and let every woman have her own husband. . . . I speak this by permission, and not of commandment. . . . For it is better to marry than to burn." It is nonetheless true that in the eyes of the Apostle, chastity and celibacy lead of themselves to the spiritual life: "He that is unmarried careth for the things that belong to the Lord, how he may please the Lord: But he that is married careth for the things that are of the world, how he may please his wife."

4. Thus exalted on the one hand as the image of divine love, but castigated on the other as the enemy of the spiritual life, tolerated ultimately but only within the limits of the strictest consecrated marriage—all the rest being left undiscussed and very summarily condemned under the labels of lust and shamelessness or "spiritual harlotry" [6]—human love was inevitably to become an endless source of problems, as much for society as for the individual. Further, linked from its origin to the reality of the person, sexual, emotional, or spiritual love (love of *bodies*, *souls*, or *minds*, according to the traditional tripartition that is, we repeat, no less Pauline than Gnostic) was thereby linked as well to the dialectic of

[6] Every religion differing from the Judaic orthodoxy is labeled a prostitution by the Prophets as by the Priests (Cf. Ezekiel 16). The exercise of the true religion or covenant can therefore find its analogy in the sexual life of spouses loyal to their oath. Similarly, the orthodoxy of the Fathers of the Church, continually on guard against spiritualist or naturalist excesses, corresponds to the curbed morality of Christian marriage, excluding both "spiritual prostitution" and the antivital asceticism of the Gnostics, who in return either reject marriage or attack it.

salvation—that is, of sin and grace—and accorded an extreme valuation. This could not happen (and has not happened) outside the Christian sphere of influence.

Hence the series of phenomena which I call eroticism, including marriage-for-love, Tristan's mystical passion, and Don Juan's impious license (the one beyond, the other this side of marriage), was to develop all its complexities only in a Europe agitated by Christian doctrine and Christian morality, from age to age in conflict with their demands (constantly more elaborately codified by the casuists)—only in a Europe formed by the Church or against it, and long identified with "Christendom." Hence we cannot interpret this phenomenon—in its development over the centuries and in its contemporary circumstance—except in the light of its religious origins and its transnatural goals.

II

THE BIRTH OF WESTERN EROTICISM

Having first appeared on the fringe of the medieval unconscious, announced under cover of symbol and myth in the twelfth century, since then secretly animating poetry and the first novels and romances (which take their name from the Romania of the troubadours), *eroticism* reaches the level of Western consciousness only at the beginning of the nineteenth century: it is the great discovery of the Romantics, who rediscover at the same time the lyricism of the troubadours and several dimensions of religious truth.

Kierkegaard, Baudelaire, and Wagner were the first to confront the consequences of this revolution with their whole being. By philosophical analysis, poetry, and music, *Either/Or*, *Les Fleurs du Mal*, and *Tristan* bear witness to a profoundly renewed awareness of the relations between human love, the life of the soul, and the spiritual quest.

For the classic writers, love raises problems only if it enters into conflict with moral duty. It is not a problem in itself. One may kill out of jealousy, or because one's (social) pride is wounded, but one cannot die of love (the metaphor itself is ridiculed). Official, unargued morality has decreed that reason should dominate the heart, and it does not worry about sex (the expression "sexual life" is still unthinkable). Instincts are classified, passions defined, and religion codified. Instincts and passions make up "the world"; to renounce the world is to enter religion. Nothing in "the world," if not the disgust one conceives for it from having abused its "pleasures" (note the word), leads to religion. Descartes, having carefully separated mind and body, no longer knows how to get them back together again: eclipse of the soul.

The radical antithesis of this classical period is given by the thinker-poets of the post-Romantic generation. For the question which their works undertake to solve is the very one that the classic writers eliminated: how to integrate human love with a religious conception of existence? Every conception of love (whether sexual or passional, libertine or matrimonial), every attitude of man confronting love, corresponds, whether consciously or not, to a spiritual attitude, expresses or betrays it, contests or assumes it, but would not exist without it. For this reason, sexuality [7] (finally recognized as something other than a "base instinct" or a simple physiological function) finds itself justified by the mind, required by the soul, dialectically related to the soul's spiritual goals. By the experience of passional love, Wagner's Isolde achieves *höchste Lust* (supreme joy). By the experience of so-called sexual love, Baudelaire's "unsatiated soul" conceives *le goût de l'éternel* (the longing for the eternal).[8] And in "In Vino Veritas," one of Kierkegaard's ironic heroes defines love as the place where "the highest spiritual life is expressed in its furthest antithesis, while sensuality claims to represent the highest spiritual life."

This new field, whose network of tensions are revealed by such phrases, determines an intermediary space between the animal body and the mind. Is this not the *soul*, in the Gnostic sense? It is, in any case, the milieu where eroticism, which is a lyrical or reflective transcendence of biological sexuality, will be able to develop all its potentialities.

These profound, anxious, or tender pleasures, moments of grace in human love and hues of mystical lan-

[7] The word appears in Kierkegaard in 1843. It had already been used by Fourier, but was then as new to the general public as nuclear energy around 1939.

[8] "Hymne," in *Les Fleurs du Mal*.

guage, proceed from the imagination. They are not, from all evidence, any more "physical" than spiritual, although they derive from both realms, and perhaps from the second most of all. They do not refer to the world of bodies, which is substantive, or to the world of the mind, which is predicative, but to the animate world of the adjective, which is qualification of substance by emotion.

In *Either/Or*, Kierkegaard shows how Christianity, by bringing into the world the "positive principle of the Spirit," which excludes the sensual, has thereby established the sensual as a "spiritual category." In other words, Christianity has raised the sexual problem and produced eroticism. Kierkegaard is not content to substitute this bipolarity for the simple duality of the classical writers. He goes on to define eroticism (in astonishingly modern terms) as "a psycho-sensual synthesis." Here eroticism is anything but a euphemism designating the sexual aspects of love in the chaste and occasionally pedantic language of Hegel's young disciple. Between the demoniac spontaneity of desire, inflamed by the mind that would deny it, and the spontaneity of amorous inclination "that recognizes as its equal only religious spontaneity"; between the contrasted figures of the Seducer and the Husband, between the negative and positive decisions of the spiritual, Kierkegaardian eroticism establishes its absolutely new problematics—"psycho-sensual," hence contained in the animistic sphere.

Now the language of the soul is none other than

myth. It is therefore natural that Kierkegaard, to describe the category of pure sensuality as the mind proposes it to attack, and Wagner, to describe pure passion as the mystical impulse transfigures it, turned to the extreme myths of Western eroticism: Don Juan, Tristan.

III

PRESENCE OF THE MYTHS AND
THEIR POWERS IN VARIOUS ORDERS

Where do the myths come from? *Are they our inventions, or are we theirs?* Do they govern our acts and our feelings, or do they appear ex post facto, as though to illustrate and qualify them, even trying to render them exemplary? Is this another chicken-and-egg problem? It would be if the myths were only poetry, that is, the invention of realities which actually exist only in their expression. But most of the myths functioning in our lives have been expressed before us, though we can be sure that some dominating us now will be expressed only tomorrow. A long duration, however, is not eternity.

The same problem is raised, moreover, with regard to the complexes and archetypes discussed by Freud, Adler, and Jung. These are not eternal Platonic ideas, cosmic laws, or categories of the mind; but are they as old as man and the circuits of his brain, or are they merely the evolved products of neolithic civilization,

spread from the Euphrates to five continents five thous-
and years before our era, the last common ancestor of
our living civilizations? Or are they specific symptoms
of our European culture alone?

At first glance, it seems easier to answer in the case of
the myths, for the dates of their emergence into world
literature are known to us, and it is from these dates on
that they have truly functioned and developed all their
contagious and revealing powers. Tristan, Faust, Hamlet,
and Don Juan are indeed the imaginative creations of
a Béroul, a Marlowe, a Shakespeare, and a Tirso de
Molina, whose co-ordinates in space and time leave
little enough margin for critical doubt. And each of
them describes the dramatic irruption of a spiritual force
into a specific society.

But another question immediately arises: have these
authors *invented* or *discovered* their characters? Have
they not simply developed the negatives of earlier or
more generally human phenomena? Here we are
brought back to the problem of the historical genesis
of the complexes. One difference, nonetheless, seems essential: the complexes and the archetypes are defined
as structures of the unconscious, while the myths speak
of the soul. Now if the conscious and the unconscious
are notions constantly relative to the degree of consciousness and of lucidity of intellect, the same is not true of
those three constituents of the human being, the body,
the soul, and the mind. If thought (which is doubt and
certainty) affords proof of the mind, and sensation that
of the body, the proof of the soul is emotion. The myths,

animistic phenomena, describe affective realities which feeling immediately perceives. And if the myths express these realities in symbols developed in a lyrical duration, and not in instantaneous concepts, thereby entering the field of consciousness under a kind of disguise that veils at the same time that it reveals them, this is not so much the result of some repression of a social, moral, or religious order (as in the case of the complexes, according to Freud) as the consequence of the very nature of the soul, whose lyrical symbol is normal language.[9]

One thing remains quite certain: the myths just cited, relatively recent in their cultural expression, are very considerably anterior to our individual problems. They have been here for several centuries, waiting for us, preforming the inner movements of our sensibility, or spreading before us the simplified images that organize our virtual adventures.[10] To meditate on the names attributed to them (and which, after the fashion of the names of the ancient gods, evoke certain groups of powers) is to meditate in fact on the structures of the soul that affect us in the manner of the stars, that is

[9] It may be true that dreams borrow from the soul its imagery, its fixed emblems, abstracted from their duration. But this is not sufficient reason to reduce the soul to the unconscious. Music is of the soul, for instance, and it does not exist before its expression; it is not held in reserve within the unconscious.

[10] Might not the myths play within the animistic a role comparable to that of the genes and genotypes which precondition the individual's susceptibility or resistance to disease? Would each of us thereby be endowed, from his birth into the cultural, intellectual, even spiritual life, with a susceptibility or a relative immunity to this or that form of erotic behavior, to this or that affective choice? Merely a hypothesis. . . .

17

to say, without determining us: *inclinant, non gubernant.*

We recognize them, at certain stages of our psychical or spiritual evolution, when we suddenly feel ourselves coincide with the form or movement of some work, poem, or story, which, long before us, had first discovered or invented them, or which, quite close to us, interprets them in terms of "modern" consciousness. A particular emotion—excitement, agony, or nostalgia, whose excess seems unusual or whose fascination secretly familiar—warns us of their appearance.

We recognize them in the great characters who have attached their fabled names to them, Oedipus or Prometheus, Tristan, Faust or Don Juan, but also in the countless descendants which these heroes have engendered deep within the works of imagination in Western literature.

And lastly, we can recognize them at work in the life of real persons, creators of art and thought, but also in the makers of history whose biographies are familiar enough to us. (Frequently the biography of an original being is his most total and continuous creation.) It is by means of, or in conflict with certain myths that the person has affirmed and recognized himself, even while contributing to their clearer expression. For the total triumph of the myth would permit only one type to subsist, thereby suppressing the individual. But this triumph is not fatal if the mind accepts the challenge and, despite the dominance of the myth which tends to imprison it in lyrical duration, pursues the history of the person, which will be the history of his freedom.

If we want to learn how the myths generally function, it seems to me that the particular study of the dominion exerted by the myths of love can help us do so best, and this for two evident reasons. The first is that the myths of love are connected with the most commonplace and widespread individual experience in our Western world: who has not been in love, or unhappy at not being so, or at least curious to know if he was? The man in the street is not tempted to see himself in Faust or Prometheus, Hamlet or Don Quixote, but does not hesitate to believe himself Don Juan if he has a taste for facility and change; or Tristan if he feels himself more inclined to love's woes, or to fidelity. The second reason is that love is linked more than any other behavior, impulse, sentiment, or ambition to its literary, musical, or plastic expression, that is, to *language* in general, but in those forms most richly endowed with popular and suggestive turns, clichés, metaphors, and accepted symbols. Love is both the best conductor and the best stimulant of expression. Similar in this (as in many other characteristics) to war in classical periods, it exists the moment it has been "declared." But it can also be brought into being by its mere evocation: by reading, by a song, an image, or a word, which are enough to induce it, or to fix its choice. Thus the action of the myths of love becomes legible insofar as it corresponds to the action of language itself.

Later, once their dynamic structures are recognized, we can rediscover the most typical among the myths in realms which appear to be independent of love and of the interplay of the sexes; realms which pass from religious or metaphysical speculation to the ethics of social action or of individual adventure. Thus I see Don Juan in the rhythm and stance of Nietzschean polemics; but also in the alternations of passionate commitment and ambiguous withdrawal (disillusion, or need to free oneself?) which characterize the career of a certain new type of thinker-adventurer in our time. I see Tristan in the intellectual passion of a Kierkegaard, whose "absolute paradox" is to "will his own destruction"; but also, as though in filigree, in the secret pattern of so many modern novels and in the "fatal" destiny of their protagonists—often unknown to their authors. And many others besides myself have seen—that is, have foreseen—Don Quixote in the magnificent madness of Christopher Columbus sailing for the Indies of his dreams.

One word more, for those who would accuse me of blaspheming—and I know such critics exist—when I see Tristan in this century. If it is true that the myths teach us as much about Europe as the statues of the animal gods or the four-armed Shivas about the civilizations of Egypt or India, they do so in the same way: not by their "realism" or by their faithfulness to everyday appearance, but by their power to express the sacred and the soul; not by their figurative, but their transfiguring value. No European has ever been Tristan or Don Juan—and no more in the past than today; yet without these myths, Europeans would not be what they are, would not love as they love, and their passions would be incomprehensible: for their passions are born of their dreams, and not of their doctrines.

IV

PROBLEMS OF THE PERSON
IN CONFLICT WITH THE MYTHS

That the myths of love generally determine our individual behavior, the apparent accidents of our encounters, and the choices we imagine we are making freely—it would be superfluous, I think, to demonstrate once again. That this action is propagated by "the culture," by the lyric or novelistic works that "impassion" us (predispose us to passion) precisely to the degree that they obey the myths, though their authors supposed they were abandoning themselves to the complete freedom of their imagination—I shall substantiate later on.

Now the myths, like laws, deal with the generic, while the person is unique or is not at all. The myths lead us to the type, while the person is the path toward an unprecedented *myself*, alone capable of a new love. The person finds the proof of his true freedom in his individual decisions, determined not by generic, pre-existing laws common to all—and which, of course, it is wise to take into account—but by a goal which is his alone, ahead of him, a goal which he achieves by approaching it, while achieving himself by this very approach.

For the person at grips with the myths, the problem will therefore consist in recognizing first their nature and their modes of action, then in being able to play with them for his own ends, or else remaining their plaything, "the puppet whose strings are pulled by an unknown force," as Kierkegaard says. In other words, the person must first of all learn to interpret the performance of the myths—in his life, in his dreams, and in the works that continue to influence him—and then try to involve in his own performance the forms of energy of which they are conductors.

This conversion of the energy of Eros will perhaps one day reveal itself as more important, for the future of humanity, than the present domestication of nuclear and solar energy. For if the latter is to permit us to explore cosmic space and to provide for the feeding of the body, the former can permit the mind to explore the little-known riches of animistic space and time, and to find in them the substance to nourish newly awakened hungers of another kind.

V

THE IRRUPTION OF EROTICISM
IN THE TWENTIETH CENTURY

Traditional Christians, lay moralists, liberal rationalists, and orthodox communists unite in deploring the irruption in our lives of an "obsessive" sexuality. The posters on street corners, in subways, and along the highways, magazines and films, detective novels, comic strips, popular songs and dances, strip tease and pin-ups—one need merely glance at the *décor* of our urban days and nights to ascertain the omnipresence of the appeal to sexual desire. This phenomenon described a thousand times remains no less stupefying in its abruptness and its scope. It dates from the first third of the twentieth century, and even if we were to find parellels for it in other times, its means of expression, at least, are unprecedented. Commercialized culture, which is its chief vehicle, renders it irreversible, and the totalitarian (or directed) cultures, though normally puritanical, will soon be overrun. Further, the quantitive and still more the qualitative increase of leisure time also increases—as Baudelaire has said with more precision than the ancient description of idleness as the mother of the vices—the practical opportunities of eroticism. To deplore the phenomenon is futile. The point is to understand its causes and above all its significance.

And first of all, we must call it by its true name. It is *eroticism* that ferments in Occidental societies, from West to East, and not sexuality strictly speaking, which is instinctual and procreative. And the means of eroticism are literature, the "dark halls" of the cinemas, the plastic arts (including photography), popular music and dances,[11] and even certain philosophies that are more

---

[11] Classical music, from Mozart to our day, is erotic; it heralds the very rare revolutions and in particular the fashions of love. It is all the more remarkable that starting from the middle of the twentieth century, experimental music abandons the realm of the animistic for that of physics and calculus, and becomes a subject for philosophical

poetic than systematic: realms par excellence in which the myths of the soul function.[12]

Hence it is with these myths, not with instinct or with "blind lust," that the mind finds itself in conflict, and with them that it can engage in a secret polemic. It is not the degree of this century's immorality that concerns it, but rather the (unconsciously religious) attitudes which justify that immorality; lastly, it is certain notions of man which an unacknowledged elite arrives at, sheltered from any social sanction: for it is here that we can discern the real meaning of the phenomenon I have referred to, and which in itself is nothing more than the foam of a tremendous tidal wave rising from the collective soul.

Behind the appearances of the street, beneath the already virtually unlimited tolerance granted to what was recently called pornography, there is something quite different from a reaction to the Victorian era, which today's youth has not experienced in its full strength and from which it cannot have suffered. It is true that a revolution never breaks out until the real tyrants are dead, and then confronts their feeble heirs,

---

engineers. Abstract painting is no less "puritanical" in appearance, but it is easier to understand its derivation from psychism: it describes a systematic introversion. Music *was* of the soul. But if it becomes the affair of specialists determined to deny the soul—that lewdness, as they call it—we are entitled to ask them what their goal is: not one has told us up till now.

[12] The mass media then spread these works to meet a pre-existing "need" which they help to make a little more demanding, while making the creators less demanding, less sincere, and all too "adjusted." But invent, in the realm of culture, and something always remains. Thus the style of present-day shop windows derives from the great surrealist exhibitions.

who protest that it is not their fault. But what was it that killed Victorian morality? Primarily, no doubt, its fear of the instinct it wanted to hold in check. Instead of justifying its rigors by describing in its reality the danger which sexual license represents for any utilitarian, labor-based society, whose highest value is not mystical union but ethical sobriety, it tried to close its eyes to the very reality of sex: to speak of it was forbidden save from the pulpit, and then only under the name of impurity. This was to drain puritan morality of its *virtù*, which was less religious, moreover, than civilizing.

Whence the effect of revelation which Freud's work produced, the impression that it "explained everything" because it explained certain problems by exactly that which no one dared mention.[13] Focusing on the guilty conscience of a bourgeoisie which no longer had the courage of its prejudices, the popularizing of psychoanalysis has done a great deal to devalue the very notions of repression and censorship. The abuses Freud exposed have made the use of the most elementary educative disciplines suspect. It is no longer license which is the enemy, but repression, that generator of complexes and neuroses. Hence the tolerance which I have referred to, and which alarms so many observers.

Before being alarmed in our turn, let us try to see clearly what happens when the official curbs weaken.

[13] Marx produces the same illuminating effect by resorting, in order to explain history, to the other repressed factor: material interest, gain, money. Let us not forget that a theory which "explains everything" still leaves each particular phenomenon, as such, to be explained.

Is it true, as we are so often told, that "sensuality invades everything" and that an unchecked sexuality "runs riot"? Of course not. Instinct does not depend on fashions, nor nature on culture—at least not so directly. What is liberated is expression, the way of talking about the subjects of love, of speculating about them or of showing them on the screen. Hence it is not sex but eroticism, not sensuality but its public avowal, its projection before our eyes, that suddenly provokes us to an awareness too long postponed. Mozart is the greatest interpreter of Don Juan, but it is not Mozart who "released" Casanova: he merely let him glimpse, toward the end, the meaning of the *dramma giocoso* of his career as a seducer. Kierkegaard, Baudelaire, and Wagner, at the height of the period of rational, puritanical, and utilitarian censorship, reveal like seismographs the subterranean movements of the repressed soul. As for today's writers, the great novelists, poets, and philosophers who are said to be "obsessed by eroticism," far from being the fomenters of the phenomenon whose obvious signs I have alluded to above, they too function as the "indicators" of what is rising to the surface of consciousness, behind these trivial appearances. Senders of messages which are still to be decoded, they advance masked by the scandal which assures their initial success; but what they thereby conceal (whether voluntarily or not) is perhaps more scandalous than what they so shamelessly show—I mean more subversive in the spiritual order than shocking to the eyes of morality. Some proclaim the fact with great solemnity. Others ignore it, or would refuse to admit it.

26

(Me, religious? You're joking!) They happen to share the prejudices of their critics, for the pleasure of violating them. Some of the most serious or revolutionary betray the symptoms of a neurosis attributable to the repression of the spiritual. Others, on the contrary, passionately profess their Gnosticism: the Eternal Feminine leads them on, toward a heaven which is not what an average Christian supposes, but the place of true spiritual thinkers. Whatever their ultimate intentions, whether avowed or disguised, whatever their "resistances to analysis" or their banal obeisance to whatever shocks and is therefore guaranteed to excite—whether they exaggerate or minimize their role—they signify something important in the development of Western culture and anthropology.

It is the eternal debate between a passionate Gnosticism and the moderating wisdom of the Church, between the personal adventure and the collective orthodoxy, which the rising tide of Eros is now renewing among us. And I do not take sides here in any general, irreversible way, for each of the terms I have just contrasted seems valid and necessary to me, though the truth is surely beyond them all, either in the resultant of their forces, as I am inclined to believe as an Occidental, or in that purified vision the Oriental writers have extolled, which would return everything to undifferentiated Unity. The essays collected in this book are not judgments against any particular thinker or any general attitude, but researches as to the nature and motives of choices typical of a person or a character, and of the style that defines them; as to the idea of man which they imply and suppose, *nolens volens*. An awareness of these motivations in concrete but exemplary cases may help us take our risks more bravely, assume our persons better.

VI

UPHEAVAL OF THE ANIMISTIC POWERS

But the sudden turbulence of Eros, before raising these problems, is primarily a great psychic fact; or at least it indicates and betokens that fact.

I am not unaware of the demographic factor—one man to every square yard in four hundred years, if all humanity continues to obey the reproductive instinct; this threat may incite us to separate still further the purely sexual from the erotic, and perhaps it is already influencing the unconscious of today's men and women; but the phenomenon that concerns us is an anterior one. Nor am I unaware of the technological factor. I believe that the mental *habitus* which it imposes upon us exaggerates the tyranny of schedules, of "measurable yield," of social discipline, and of rational behavior in general to such a degree that a revolution of the soul becomes inevitable, by way of compensation: will the invasion of our lives by technology provoke that "outburst of eroticism" which would tend to neutralize its dehumanizing effects? We can imagine such a thing statistically, but not verify it in our personal lives.

Must we therefore accept the hypothesis of a collective soul which has its own life, and which wields over men a power comparable to the action of the moon upon the ocean and the bodies of women? But what is the soul?

I do not take the word in the vague, noble sense, and still less in the religious sense that so many of our common expressions give it, such as "good soul" or "salvation of the soul" or "immortality of the soul" (designating the person or the spirit), but in the much more exact sense which its derivatives such as *animation, animosity, animadversion* still preserve. The *animated* performance of a musician manifests by psychical means a reality which is neither material nor strictly spiritual, which is not of the body or of the intellect, but rather of the "heart," as we say—of the soul.

The soul is the realm of the impulses that transcend the demands of instinct and conflict with the decrees of society. It is also the realm of those passions which counteract the "programs" of physiological life recorded by our chains of chromosomes, which contradict the anticipations of economy and disturb our systems of rational and spiritual communications, in the manner of solar explosions. Too long neglected or denied by Western thought, which took only mind and body seriously, the animistic forces are in full offensive in the twentieth century. Their first manifestations were of course anarchic, neurotic, or pathological: the tidal wave initially projects nothing but mud. Revolutions and collective delirium on the political and social level; discredit of laws and conventions of every kind, racism, the enormous popularity of superstition and the magic of charlatans —that is the mud. The tidal wave of eroticism comes next, still turbulent and tumultuous. If the dikes have collapsed, it is because they were too weak for a new pressure that is suddenly too great. We must now invent a new system of canals to transform the inundation into a life-giving irrigation.

It is love which is once again called into question— all love: sexual or passional, normal or aberrant, matrimonial or spiritual. "Love has to be reinvented," Rimbaud said. This kind of psychic revolution has only one precedent in the history of Western culture: it is located, in the most precise manner, in the twelfth century.

Since the end of the Roman Empire, no original love poems or treatises on mysticism had been written. Sexual life seemed reduced to an obscure animality. Marriage raised only problems of inheritance and consanguinity that were often preposterous, justifying divorces caused by interest but never by sentiment. And suddenly here are the troubadours and the invention of sublimated desire, Saint Bernard of Clairvaux and the mysticism of love, Héloïse and passion in experience, Tristan and passion in dream, the cult of the Lady, the cult of the Virgin, the revival of the Gnostic heresies, libertine cynicism in its embryonic state, the celibacy of priests, and the *Lois d'Amour*—in short, lyricism, eroticism, and mysticism unleashed over all of Europe, and speaking one and the same new language, revitalizing for centuries to come both music and poetry, the novel, piety, and manners. All this occurred within cultivated elites—the jongleurs and the preaching monks being the only "means of diffusion" permitting such things to reach the people. This first great revolution of love, so sudden in its explosion, was slow to propagate its revolutionary effects in the manners and mental habits of the uneducated masses. The labor of decantation, of psychological adaptation, and of a moral and spiritual reorganization was to take centuries, and is not over.

For the revolution that we are living through renews in part that of the twelfth century, submerges some of its conquests, but is much broader in its total effect. It explodes in a society much less partitioned and protected, where every pulsation that can be recorded is immediately propagated. Cheap printing, the films, radio, and television leave no more delays or dead spots. *The effects reach our senses before the causes have emerged in our consciousness.* Hence the scandal, to put it mildly —hence the anxiety and the bad conscience which characterize both those who express the revolution and those who are suffering its effects.

Take a cultivated European—man or woman—raised according to bourgeois morality, whether a believer or not, more or less deferential to science and progress, in other words normal and average according to the century's standards; confront him with the works, published in the last fifty years, of Freud and the schools that derive from him, of Proust and Joyce, of D. H. Lawrence and Jean Genet, of André Breton and Robert

31

Musil, of Henry Miller and Lawrence Durrell, to cite
only a very few of the most celebrated names; add the
celebrated *Histoire d'O*, the essays of Georges Bataille
and Pierre Klossowski for the initiates; detective novels
of the Spillane-Chandler type, and the films of the inter-
national New Wave for the general public. What will
the normal and average witness see in all this at first
sight? The libido in ferment everywhere, neurosis taken
as a standard theme, the negation of innocence, even in
childhood; primitive coupling or, on the contrary, the
most unwonted passion exalted as true purity; sadism
and masochism; homosexuality and incest; and every
form of exhibitionism and perverse refinement still to
be given names; in short, lust, anxious or complacent,
sophisticated or commercial, not only studied but justified! How would our witness distinguish in all this
anything but an enormous depravity, a lack of control
but also of lightness, of real tenderness but also of *saine
gauloiserie?* And how could he regard it as an "up-
heaval of the soul," a return of the spirit, as certain
aberrant minds dare to call it? Can we tell him that
there is indeed more than pederasty in Proust, incest
in Musil, lust in Miller, or simple coitus in love? He sees
first what shocks him, which is also what tempts him.
Confronted with the "indiscipline of manners" and the
"pornography" which would be its cause, he feels out-
raged and distressed. If he is serious, if he sees further,
his feelings may reach the point of anxiety.

Now these tendencies happen to be *the same* as those
of the erotic authors, although these latter have inverse

motives for outrage, distress, or anxiety. The two camps scorn each other, and each refuses to tolerate even momentarily, as a simple hypothesis of dialogue, whatever good arguments the other might raise.

It is from this point that I am trying to reflect, to elucidate love as it is written about in my time.

VII

DIGRESSION ON THE MEANING
OF WORDS

As the key signature of this Introduction I should have liked to set a sign of objectivity, announcing that here the writer describes before judging. Let it therefore remain understood that in these prefatory pages and in the essays that follow I never use the terms *bourgeois morality* and *puritanical* as insults, nor as necessarily depreciative. On the other hand, the word *eroticism* does not define either good or evil for me, but an emotional phenomenon par excellence, concerning which I am trying, before evaluating it, to see more clearly its nature, its source, and its goal.

I understand why contemporary literature scorns the puritanical and identifies it with madness, stigmatizing it as both ridiculous and dangerous. But I am not forgetting that without the sexual discipline which the so-called puritanical tendencies have imposed upon us since Europe first existed, there would be nothing more in our civilization than in those nations known as underdeveloped, and no doubt less: there would be neither work, organized effort, nor the technology which has created the present-day world. There would also not be the problem of eroticism! The erotic authors forget this fact quite naively, committed as they are to their poetic or moralizing passion, which too often alienates them from the true nature of the "facts of life" and their complex links with economy, society, and culture.

On the other hand, without eroticism and the freedom it supposes, would our culture be worth more than that which a Stalin, a Mao have attempted to impose by decree? It would be strictly adapted to material production, to socialized procreation. And this our puritans forget no less often.

Hence I am posing a problem that is concrete to the highest degree, and which the understandable anxiety of the West today generally tends to settle quite ruthlessly before having even considered it.

VIII

TOWARD A MYTHANALYSIS OF CULTURE

Erotic literature contains more psychological realities than bourgeois morality chose to accept, and than puritanism tolerates. Yet these realities, however they are judged, are at least as ordinary and obsessive as the economic realities which moreover depend on them to a certain degree, as our notion of comfort depends on our psychology.

34

Once recognized, they raise problems for us which will no longer be solved by being denied. The discoveries of depth analysis, the relaxation of sexual taboos, the increase of comfort and leisure, birth control, mass media—all function in the same irreversible direction. It is apparent that by calling into question the entire spectrum of personal and social, ethical and spiritual relationships which constitute love, erotic literature is reacting to phenomena which it has not provoked, which indeed transcend it, but whose still chaotic demands it attempts to formulate and illustrate. It is also apparent that we can emerge from the inevitable chaos caused by so rapid a development only by advancing, not by turning back to the disciplines of earlier periods. But first of all, how can we order our research and reflection?

I have chosen two methods of analysis, of which several new or renewed applications will be found in this book:

1) To seek out the religious and philosophical equivalents of the attitudes described or extolled by contemporary literature dealing with love; and to discover how these attitudes are related (or not related) to certain fundamental conceptions of man as defined by the great religions, by their metaphysics, and by their heresies.

Love in the Western World illustrated this approach, starting from a line of reasoning whose outline I summarize here: eroticism begins where sexual emotion becomes, beyond its procreative goal, an end in itself or an instrument of the soul; now the Gnostic and Mani-

35

chean beliefs do not decry sexual pleasure and do not
discourage passion, quite the contrary; what they decry
is procreation, by which one angel more is enclosed in
a vile body; eroticism, actually an invention of the
twelfth century, has therefore every likelihood of corresponding to Gnostic and Manichean religious attitudes,
and the judgments that might be passed upon it translate a spiritual configuration for or against these attitudes, whether consciously or not; and the more consciously the better.

Evidently the point is to *make explicit* religious elements generally repressed or quite simply unrealized.
A method exactly the inverse of Freud's, but thereby
comparable to his.

2) To learn how to read in filigree the play of the
myths in the obscure complexities and the apparently
insane involvements of contemporary eroticism.

Between the sciences of the body and of the mind,
between biology and theology, beyond the necessities
of the species but this side of good and evil, without
laws or dogmas, but not without symbols governing
our emotive life, mythology performs its function—
which is a function of the soul.

Great simple and organizing forms, active symbols
and vehicles of the animistic powers of Eros, the myths
can serve us as guides in the infernal, purgatorial, or
sublime comedy of our desires, our passions, our love.
When we are ignorant of their nature, they rule us
pitilessly and lead us astray. But to identify them, to
learn their language and the gestures habitual to them

can permit us to find the scarlet thread in the labyrinth we are lost in, and to orient ourselves in the dark wood of our fantasies, toward an issue of light and our true desire.

I propose a *mythanalysis*, which can be applied not only to persons but to the characters of art, and to certain formulations of life; the immediate objective of such a method being to elucidate the motives of our choices and their too frequently unconscious implications, spiritual as well as social.

We shall then find ourselves facing the real ethical and religious problem, the one that requires a decision or a risk: must we believe that freedom can be mastered only by the *detachment* of our relations with the flesh, with the world, and with our individual self? Or must we rather *order* these relations toward the supreme goal, which prompts the *person* within us?

We are in the world as though not of the world, but rather as destined continually to transform it (whence technology) for other tasks that transcend and at the same time create us. From this I deduce that our vocation is indeed to proceed elsewhere, but with all that we are; and that such a vocation is less an *ascesis* than a transmutation; not a flight but an awareness, an awareness of ourselves and of the world, in the name of a sense which is proper and exclusive to us, and by which we achieve the universal.

To deny the myths and their dominion would be disastrous. To attempt to escape them by charging them with error—whether theological or rational—is an illusory enterprise. The point is to understand and feel their powers, then to treat them as it is suitable for man to treat Nature: he can command her only by first obeying her laws and structures.

When we are better acquainted with the myths that tempt us, when we know whence they come and where their logic leads, perhaps we shall be in a better position to take our personal risk, to assume our love and proceed toward ourselves. Perhaps we shall be a little more free.

NEW METAMORPHOSES
OF TRISTAN

Passion is that form of love which refuses the immediate, avoids dealing with what is near, and if necessary invents distance in order to realize and exalt itself more completely. This definition covers most real novels, by which I mean not the best works conventionally classed in this literary genre but—independent of their artistic quality, their notoriety, or their human scope—only those works in which the medieval archetype of *Tristan* prevails.

I cannot decide whether passion derives from distance, or distance from passion. What is certain is that up to now the Western novel has never described a passion kindled for an object near at hand, easily accessible, and morally sanctioned or even generally tolerated. Though the nature and number of these subsisting tolerances and prohibitions vary according to the society in question (which can be characterized by its taboos: for instance, the Victorian bourgeois reluctance to discuss money or sex, and the consequent shock of revelation produced by Marx and Freud), passion, which is always antisocial, nonetheless receives its objects from society itself—and from society alone, by a fine paradox—these objects differing according to the existing state of mores.

No passion is conceivable or in fact declared in a world where everything is permitted. For passion always presupposes, between subject and object, a third party constituting an obstacle to their embrace—a King Mark separating Tristan from Iseult—the obstacle being social (moral, conventional, even political) to such a degree that we even find it identified, at its limit, with society itself, though it is generally represented by a *dramatis persona,* in accord with the requirements of narrative, the rhetoric of romance.

In a society like ours, can passion still find *prohibitions* severe and consequently fascinating enough to enable its frenzy to declare itself? I intend to speak of Western society, that is, of Europe and its extensions in America and Russia; a society fermented and formed by an age-old quarrel between the Sacred, creator of taboos, and the Profane, born of their violation; but also between Wisdom and Policy, Grace and Merit, Mysticism and Morality, Belief and Science, Absolute and Reason, and lastly between Passion and Marriage. Are we not at that point in our social evolution where—all things being reduced ("coming down to," as we say), profaned, scrubbed clean of religious, neurotic, or emotional illusions, and subject, by the intermediary of increasingly indiscreet analyses, to the rules of hygiene and sociology —*everything seems permitted* that will not harm health and productivity? (Everything else, moreover, being increasingly banned.)

Some twenty years ago, when I was writing *Love in*

the Western World, I foresaw that a culture too aware of its ends and means, in other words too sociological, would leave no room for passion as it was invented in the twelfth century by the Languedoc troubadours and elaborated by the Bretons. My anticipation relied too heavily on the moral taboos of the Victorian and bourgeois period, and on the successes of the psychoanalysts and the Marxists who have been living on these taboos for over half a century. Other taboos subsist, or have been reconstituted, on which passion flings itself to find new pretexts for gloriously consuming itself, for defying Daylight morality in the name of Night's mysticism, and the life of rational action in the name of ecstasy and rapturous death.

I

THREE NOVELS OF PASSION
IN THE TWENTIETH CENTURY

Three major works in which the Tristan archetype appears have been produced toward the middle of this century by Europe, America, and Russia. Of each one might say, with some justification, that it was "really" a social, moral, or political description of Imperial Austria, of the United States, or of the Revolution and its consequences in Russia. But each can also be described as the last novel of passion in Western literature. Boris Pasternak's *Doctor Zhivago* is not a political act, according to Camus, but on the contrary "a great book of love." Lionel Trilling's essay on Vladimir Nabokov's *Lolita* is called "The Last Lover." And the heroine of Robert Musil's *The Man Without Qualities* says on several occasions, referring to herself and her brother: "We'll have been the last romantics of love. . . . Actually, ours is the last love story possible. . . . We'll probably be the last of love's Mohicans."

I am not concerned with literary criticism here, my only intention being to illustrate a theme to whose fatal glamour I am obviously not the last to respond. Need I assert that this great theme is the sole justification of my essay? The myth of passion aside, everything distinguishes the three works I am about to consider. And I am only too aware of the likelihood that their mere juxtaposition may shock the reader's aesthetic sense and outrage his moral sensibility. But it is also possible that the incongruity of such a comparison will serve a purpose: the more discrepant (in every regard *save one*) the three works considered, the more significant the action of the myth which they reveal, and which is their only common measure. I shall therefore concern myself, in these three works, only with the appearance of Tristan, imperiously dictating—unknown to the authors—the profound rhetoric of their composition.

Let us proceed with the experiment without further precautions. Here are the archetypical résumés for all three novels, as their authors themselves might have furnished them, had they accepted my hypothesis and adopted the angle of vision I propose:

44

VLADIMIR NABOKOV. In the eyes of the "old European" I happen to be from birth, America is a welcoming homeland, rather than an exile. The reader will realize that I love America, despite all that irritates me about her, and despite what she wants to be, what she believes she is. Her perverse immaturity fascinates me. The scandalous hero (by antiphrasis) of my novel (educated in Europe, as I make quite explicit) espouses the American way of life (in the person of a thoroughly middle-class matron) only out of an obsessional love for her daughter. But this is an impossible love as well, for Lolita is not yet thirteen. Nonetheless, my hero kidnaps and flees with her, from hotel to motel, across the entire American continent which he thus discovers and matchlessly describes, at the same time that he finds himself rejected by the social milieu, its laws and its conventions. Abandoned by his nymphet, he commits a lunatic crime and dies drunk with love in his prison, after having written this posthumous book.

ROBERT MUSIL. I cherished my "royal and imperial" Austria with an exigent, lucid, and ironical love. But she belonged to a social milieu, to a political and cultural elite that, both decadent and conventional, was to abandon her to war, then to worse. I have said so in an enormous novel whose central character, Ulrich von X (who resembles me like a brother), transfers his passion, which has been frustrated by reality, to his own sister, that is, to the only "neighbor" in his country whom he manages to love "as himself." But this neighbor is "forbidden" by morality. Loving his sister, Ulrich desires to possess the inaccessible which, if it offers access to a life of ecstasy, cuts him off from social life. My hero becomes an exile in his own country, as I have become an exile *tout court*.[1]

BORIS PASTERNAK. I passionately love my Russia and desire to be loved by her, as Doctor Zhivago loves Lara and is loved by her. But like Lara, Russia has had to obey a cynical and brutal Master who seduced and humiliated her. He forbids me to speak to her. I nonetheless tell her of my love under the mask of a novel full of allusions and symbols which she will understand. And the world turns my declaration of love into a triumph! The Master immediately claims I have insulted Russia. In the name of my beloved he rejects and threatens to exile me. But such is my love that I can lie: I shall ask the tyrant's pardon, begging him to let me live a little longer beside my beloved who is forced to turn from me, for away from her my life has no meaning, it is near her that I wish to keep silence.

Thus reduced to their mythic diagram—the characters in the drama are easily recognizable, these Tristans separated from an Iseult "forbidden" by a King Mark who is Morality, Society, or the Regime—these three novels reveal the same ambiguity as to the true nature if not of their subject, at least of the chief interest they

[1] Musil died in Geneva in 1942, in great poverty.

afford the reader: criticism of a society or chronicle of a passion?

During the Renaissance, there was a vogue for fantastic landscapes which, turned at a certain angle, suddenly revealed the features of a human head. It is the inverse phenomenon that occurs upon reading these three novels: you stare a long time at this woman's face and a landscape, a country, a whole society gradually appears before you, recomposes itself and invades the entire canvas. You continue reading and no, it was really a woman all along. What has the author meant? All that we see here, no doubt, and more. If he could have said so otherwise, he would have done so (and we would not be reading him). But the writer's answer is not enough, however sincere.

For we must see that this ambiguity, which he propounds in spite of himself, is not at all accidental. It does not result, I insist, from some prolonged hesitation on the author's part between two central themes, or two literary genres, or two spheres of imagination. It expresses and irresistibly translates the fundamental ambiguity of passion, antisocial by definition, hence linked to the social milieu by a permanent strife without which it would not exist, and for which this very milieu limits the occasion, dictates the object, or furnishes the pretext; as will be shown by the application to all three novels of the mythological analysis proposed in *Love in the Western World*.

II

LOLITA, OR SCANDAL

"Between the age limits of nine and fourteen there occur maidens who, to certain bewitched travelers, twice or many times older than they, reveal their true nature, which is not human, but nymphic (that is, demoniac); and these chosen creatures I propose to designate as 'nymphets.'" Lolita, twelve years and seven months old, has the disturbing charm, the innocent shamelessness, and the touch of vulgarity that characterize the nymphet. Humbert Humbert, a European in his late thirties, who has been in America only a short time, discovers her in a small town where he is taking his vacation. Love at first sight. Lunatic plot to possess the child, whose mother he marries first. This unfortunate creature soon dies, run over by an automobile. H.H. takes Lolita away with him to a hotel called The Enchanted Hunters. He gives her a sleeping pill, but dares not take advantage of her slumbers. In the morning, it is she who seduces him! Then begins the long flight of the stepfather and daughter, tracked by their secret guilt, across the entire expanse of the United States,[2] until the day Lolita escapes, seduced by another middle-aged man whom Humbert will eventually kill. At seventeen, married to a brawny young mechanic, she dies in childbed, a few

[2] This "geographic" part of the book suggests a parody of Nils Holgersson's journey across Sweden.

48

weeks after Humbert, who is spared capital punishment by a coronary thrombosis.

I do not mean to veil or to excuse the novel's scandalous character, for it appears to be essential, and the author misses no opportunity to underline and accentuate it, either by reproaching his hero in a preface attributed, moreover, to an American psychiatrist; or, more convincingly, by the cynical flippancy of Humbert Humbert's style. If loving nymphets was not, in our day and age, one of the last surviving sexual taboos (with incest), there would be neither true passion nor true novel, in the "Tristanian" sense of these terms. For the necessary obstacle would be missing between the two protagonists, the necessary *distance* by which the mutual attraction, instead of being mitigated or exhausted by sensual gratification, is metamorphosed into passion. It is first and foremost the evident scandal, the profaning character of H.H.'s love for Lolita that betrays the presence of the myth.

Let us leave aside for the moment the profound differences that separate this ironic and witty novel from the somber epic of a Béroul, so simple and immediate in its effects. We must not overlook the fact that the story of Tristan was no less shocking to the twelfth century than *Lolita* is today.

What habit and anachronistic illusion, assisted by Bédier's modern version, make us accept all too easily as the touching story of an almost chaste love that happened to be conceived out of wedlock, actually concealed revolutionary powers for readers of the period. The first versions of Tristan glorified a form of love not only opposed to marriage but unable to exist save outside it. They "justified" [3] in the name of this new love a whole series of actions regarded as crimes: blasphemous stratagem of the rigged trial-by-ordeal, repeated violation of allegiances and sworn faith, profanation of the feudal oath and of the Catholic sacraments, witchcraft, black magic. All this against a background of heresy much more dangerous at the time than are modern youth's extravagances, ephemeral fashions that seem to profit press and cinema more than they prey on society.

On the other hand, passionate love for a still impubescent girl would not have seemed surprising in the Middle Ages. It is customary to venerate Dante's love for Beatrice, who was nine years old, and Petrarch's for Laura, who was twelve; these two examples establish a tradition of high European literature, which will be illustrated at closer range by Goethe creating the character of Mignon, Novalis dedicating his work to the love of Sophie von Kühn, who died at sixteen, Edgar Allan Poe marrying a girl of fourteen, and especially by the inspired Lewis Carroll: *Alice in Wonderland* is the product of nymphet-love suppressed by the clergyman's conscience but avowed by some of his poems and betrayed by the often savage jokes in his letters to little girls.

[3] In an implicit or masked fashion in Béroul and Thomas, explicit and aggressive in Gottfried von Strassburg, whom Wagner took as the source of his inspiration.

Adultery today leads only to divorce or exhausts itself in commonplace liaisons. It no longer offers a
serious support to what Freud once called the *élan
mortel*, secret of Tristanian love. And the absence of
the sacred dims the passions, which awareness of a
profanation once caused to burn so brightly. We are left
with two sexual taboos, strangely respected by our
mores in rapid transition from a primitive sense of the
sacred to a scientific hygiene: nymphet-love and incest.
Are these two loves *contra naturam?* We find them
widely practiced in the animal world and in the great
majority of human societies, the Western bourgeoisie
constituting the most notable exception. Such practices
are less against nature than against civilization. "I found
myself maturing amid a civilization which allows a man
of twenty-five to court a girl of sixteen but not a girl
of twelve." Humbert describes, at the beginning of his
memoirs, the love he conceived at the age of thirteen
for a child of twelve whom he called Annabel and who
died soon after—an evocation of Poe. Thus the Eros
of this adult, otherwise sexually normal male is fixated
on the child-woman, rendered doubly inaccessible by
the difference in age and by the idea of death. This is
how the nymphet becomes the mainstay of passion—
that is, of the infinite desire which escapes the natural
rhythms and plays the role of an absolute preferable to
life itself. The possession of this inaccessible object then
becomes ecstasy, "the supreme joy," the *höchste Lust*
of the dying Isolde.

Yet those who have read *Lolita* with more perverse

amusement than emotion will be entitled to suspect the legitimacy of so solemn an interpretation.

Of course, from the initial *coup de foudre* to the death of the separated lovers—the consequence of a forbidden love that exiles them from the community and consumes without truly uniting them—the great moments of the Myth are easily identifiable. Has the author been aware of them? Certain episodes of the novel would suggest that this was the case, allusions to the most typical situations and peripeties of the Tristan legend. But it is curious to note that on each occasion a touch of irony accompanies the allusion. Thus the hero's mother dies very early (as in Tristan), but this is the tone of the narrative: "My very photogenic mother died in a freak accident (picnic, lightning) when I was three." (We remember the lugubrious tone of fate, the *alte Weise* that marks the mother's death in *Tristan!*) The name of the hotel where the seduction occurs, The Enchanted Hunters, obviously recalls the state of trance of the avowal scene in *Tristan,* but the entire description of the place aims precisely at disenchanting it. The episode of the love-philter is present, but made absurd by its failure: it is only a sleeping pill which H.H. makes Lolita take by a ruse, and which moreover turns out to be too weak, the doctor who provided it having erred as to its ingredients or having bilked his client. (A point-by-point and probably deliberate inversion of the account of Brangaene's "fatal" error.) As in *Tristan,* it is true, the attack on marriage in the name of passion animates the entire narrative. As in *Tristan,* we feel that the author is not interested by the sexual aspect of his story, but solely by the magic of Eros, and he says as much: "I am not concerned with so-called (sex) at all. Anybody can imagine those elements of animality. A greater endeavor lures on: to fix once and for all the perilous magic of nymphets." As in *Tristan*, "the lovers flee the world, and the world them." Lastly, as in *Tristan*, they die within a short time of one another, separated. But their death is as sordid as the death of the legendary lovers was triumphant in the twelfth-century and Wagnerian versions.

This is because in reality H.H. and Lolita have never known what I call "unhappy reciprocal love." Lolita has never responded to the fierce and tender passion of her elder lover. Hence the failure of the Myth and the "savagely facetious" tone of the novel, its pitiless realism and its somewhat mad jokes saved (just barely, on occasion) from vulgarity by a dazzling verbal virtuosity. If Lolita had loved the narrator, if she had been his Iseult, the realistic novel would have given way to the poem, and the social satire to an inner lyricism. The hypothesis is not an arbitrary one, for this is precisely what happens in Musil's great book, as we shall see. But the absence, here very striking, not only of any kind of emotional impurity, but also of any spiritual horizon, reduces the novel to the dimensions of a genre-study of mores in the manner of Hogarth. We share the author's irritations, we acclaim his syntax and his vocabulary, we laugh often, we are never moved.

Such as it is, this perfect work remains, too, a

Tristan manqué. And this is consonant with the immaturity of the very object of the passion described; yet without this immaturity there would be no obstacle, hence no passion. Perhaps the book, after all, is vicious only with regard to this circle.

III

ROBERT MUSIL AND THE
"MILLENNIAL KINGDOM"

Engineer, officer, philosopher, writer, religious spirit in spite of himself, since he was in search of a truth to live by, Robert Musil died virtually unknown, in the city where I am writing about him, and his work, in part posthumous, will continue to rise on the horizon of European literature. The devastating comedy, the calm lucidity, the lyricism that wells from it despite the acuity of a constantly critical attention, the infinitely diversified investigation of human relationships, of social roles, of the problems of love and the goals of life confer on the two thousand pages of his last work [4] a spellbinding power I had not experienced since Proust's work, which is more polished, no doubt, and of infinitely easier access, but of a lesser spiritual virtue. I should have enjoyed writing about Musil, but about him alone. And I feel some scruples at making him figure in a context he transcends, particularly since I am here con-

[4] *Der Mann ohne Eigenschaften*, translated as *The Man Without Qualities*.

cerned to discuss his endless masterpiece solely from the viewpoint of passion. Fortunately, Musil has described this para-mystical tendency in a language rich in correspondences with that of my analyses of the Myth, and with a precision so constant that I can frequently substitute quotation for commentary. But a still more curious coincidence serves my undertaking: I discover that Musil not only twice touches on the theme of a passionate love for a child, but chooses to see in it a prefiguration of the forbidden love that will unite his hero and heroine: Ulrich and Agathe, brother and sister. An admirable coincidence, which we must certainly attribute to the logic of the Myth, in the absence of any other element that authorizes the comparison of two works so disparate in climate and ambition.

Ulrich von X is talking to his sister Agathe, whom he realizes he is beginning to love, and describes, without quite knowing why, this recollection:

"It was in a streetcar. A little girl got on, she was perhaps twelve years old, accompanied by a very young father or her elder brother. From her way of walking into the car, of sitting down, of casually holding out the money for two fares to the conductor, you could see she was a lady already, but without a hint of childish affectation. . . . She was marvelously beautiful: dark, her lips full, her eyebrows strong, her nose slightly *retroussé:* a brunette Pole maybe, or a southern Slav. . . . One can fall passionately, mortally in love with such an apparition, without the slightest trace of lust being involved. I remember having glanced timidly at the other riders, because I had the impression that everyone was avoiding me. Then I got off behind the child, and lost her in the crowd. . . ." "How do you reconcile that" [Agathe asks] "with the fact that love no longer exists, that only sexuality and friendship remain?" "It can't be reconciled at all!" [Ulrich exclaims, laughing.]

We see that love-as-passion is the exclusive concern here, and that the only example of it the hero finds is that of the "mortal" attraction to a nymphet.

On another occasion, again telling his sister about the "ineffable" forms of love which, moreover, he regards as expressing "deficient and strained relations with the world," Ulrich repeats the story of the "most marvelous woman he has ever found in his path": "She ravished him like a love poem written in secret, whose allusions are steeped in a still unknown happiness. . . ." "Is it not against nature to transfer such emotions to a child?" Agathe asks. "Only a clumsily directed lust would be against nature," Ulrich answers. "The man who would be capable of such a thing would involve the creature, disarmed and still incomplete, in problems she is not equipped to face. He should abstract the immaturity of this body and this mind in formation, acting out his passion with a mute and hidden partner. . . .[5] That is an entirely different attitude, with entirely different results!" And, as he still senses a kind of reprobation, perhaps a jealous censure, from Agathe, he adds: "If I

[5] Elsewhere, Musil returns to this theme: "A partner of unequal value unbalances love; only it should be added that often it is an imbalance of emotion that involves the choice of such an object." See my remark on the vicious circle of Lolita.

have told this story, it is because it is a preface to the love between brother and sister."

I need not italicize the revealing phrases in the context of our analysis: everything would have to be underlined! Not only do these two pages suggest a penetrating criticism of *Lolita*, but they introduce a dialogue that leads to the heart of the drama of passion:

"Love between brother and sister?" Agathe asks, as if she were hearing this phrase for the first time. . . . Ulrich adds abruptly:

> "The man whose strongest excitations are linked to experiences which are all impossible in one manner or another, refuses the experiences which *are* possible! It may be that the imagination is a flight from life, a refuge for cowardice and a cavern of vices, as many claim. I think that the story of the little girl, and all the other examples we have mentioned, far from being the result of monstrosity or weakness, reveal a refusal of the profane, an insubordination, an excessive and excessively passionate desire for love!"

The impossible experience in which Ulrich is engaged first occurs to him in the form of a need for love "freed of the social and sexual countercurrents and aversions": "He dreamed of a woman who would be absolutely inaccessible. She floated before his eyes like those late-autumn days in the mountains, when the air has something bloodless, something moribund about it, while the colors burn at the extreme limit of passion."

With this reverie mingles the image of his sister

Agathe, encountered after long years of absence, and who, fleeing her husband, comes to live in Ulrich's little rococo mansion surrounded by its superb grounds in Vienna.

> Often, even during the years when Ulrich had sought his way alone and not without insolence, the word *sister* had been charged for him with a vague nostalgia, though it would never have occurred to him at the time that he possessed a real and living sister. . . . No doubt analogous phenomena are frequent. In more than one life, an imaginary sister is only the juvenile, ineffable form of a need for love which later, once the dreams have faded, contents itself with a bird, an animal of some kind, or turns toward humanity and one's "neighbor."

From Chateaubriand to D'Annunzio and Thomas Mann, by way of French, German, and English romanticism, we can follow the literary fortunes of this form of forbidden love; it would be curious to discover why the period during which Musil's novel takes place—the eve of the First World War—was the last in which it flourished.

The slow and fascinating story of the growing awareness, and then of the choice of this love by two beings in every way normal, extraordinarily intelligent, integrated into the social life of a European capital but irritated by its insignificance, fills the second part of this enormous novel. The wealth of skillful descriptions, the pitiless humor of the reflections exchanged by brother and sister, the quality of their moral demands and their spiritual nostalgias compose a philter of an effectiveness unequaled

in contemporary literature. It is not *René*, it is not Byron,
it is neither decadent nor scandalous. Perhaps it is less a
matter of incest than of relations between Animus and
Anima, as the commentators suggest. For me, it is only a
matter of passion—that is, of a fundamental secret of the
European psyche. Incest here is only the actual condition
of the "last possible love story," and of an admirable
analysis of the spiritual specter haunting the West.

Here is the dialectic of Eros and Agapè, the struggle
between the impulse that bears man toward the angel,
and the need to love others, basis of all society. "With a
relative objectivity, he admitted that the relations between Agathe and himself had involved, from the beginning, a large proportion of aversion for society. . . ."
And Musil, in a note for one of the unfinished chapters,
adds:

> The man who tends toward God, according to Adler,
> is the man who is deprived of a sense of community—ac-
> cording to Schleiermacher, is the man who is indifferent
> to morality. . . . I must love you (Agathe thinks) be-
> cause I cannot love others. God and the antisocial. From
> the beginning, her love for Ulrich has mobilized her hos-
> tility toward the world.

The moment that denies world and society—a moment inherent in all true passion—appears, however, to
those who experience it as only an accessory consequence. They want to *burn*. And they believe they discover, at the most dissimilar periods, that it is the present
state of society which condemns passion and stoops to
marriage.

Our age, which has probably lost the notion of amorous passion, because the latter is more religious than sexual, considers it childish to be preoccupied with love, and expends all its efforts on marriage, whose natural *processus* it analyzes with meticulous vigor. Already a number of books have been published which speak (with all the brave candor of a gymnastics instructor) of the "revolutions of sexual life" and attempt to help men to be married and still content. Such works regard man and woman as no more than "bearers of the male or female seed" or even "sexual partners," and baptize as a "sexual problem" the boredom they attempt to banish from their relations by every kind of physical or psychical variant.

But the need for passion, confronting social prohibition, immediately projects its own nostalgia for an *infinite* desire upon it, even calling this projection destiny. This, then, is the dialectic of pure Tristanian passion gathering way: themes of *the look*, of *the storm*, and of *the sword of chastity* between two bodies:

> When their eyes met, there was then only one certitude between them: that everything was decided and that all prohibitions were now indifferent to them. . . . Each breath published their complicity; defying everyone, they suffered that common need to free themselves at last from the sadness of desire, though suffering it was so sweet that the images of fulfillment had already united them in their imagination, as the storm whips up the waves into a veil of foam; a still mightier need enforced calm upon them, and they were incapable of touching each other again.

The essential ambiguity between love projected onto the other and the refusal of the possession that would end

desire, explains the choice of a forbidden object, ceaselessly recreating the distance necessary to the troubadours' "*l'amour de loin*." Yet what is this desire? Is it a
desire for the other, or merely desire in itself? Musil's
hero and heroine speak of it with a kind of Goethean lucidity that is even somewhat didactic in places:

> "To say: I love *you* is to make a confusion. One be-
> lieves one loves *you*, this person who has provoked one's
> passion and whom one can take in one's arms, whereas
> one really loves the person provoked by the passion, that
> barbarous idol which is not the same thing at all!" "Ac-
> cording to you," [Agathe says] "one would have to be-
> lieve that one really loves only an unreal person?" "That
> is the heart of the matter: in all external relationships,
> the real person must represent the imagined person and
> even merely coincide with that person. Hence the count-
> less confusions which give the naive dealings of love so
> fascinating a spectral character."

This is why the passion-struck lovers always invoke
the Platonic myth of the two halves of the single being
that are seeking each other:

> "This desire for a double of the other sex that resem-
> bles us absolutely while still being other, for a magical
> creature who is ourself while possessing the advantage,
> over all our imaginings, of an autonomous existence. . . .
> We find traces of it in even the most banal circumstances
> of love: in the attraction linked to any change, any dis-
> guise, as in the importance of unison and the repetition
> of self in the other. . . . The great, the implacable amo-
> rous passions are all linked to the fact that a being imag-
> ines he sees his most secret self spying upon him behind
> the curtain of another's eyes."

Whence the illusion that the Self is abolished in this Night of indistinction celebrated in the second act of *Tristan:* "The shining night enfolds all contradictions within its maternal arms and upon its heart; there is no longer a true word or a false one, each word being the incomparable birth of the spirit, that which man knows in the invention of a thought. . . . On such nights, the Self keeps nothing within itself . . . the exalted identity is radiant in an infinite self-oblivion of itself. . . ." But Agathe says a little later: "Why don't you know a philter against what, at the last moment, separates us?"

But at this point Musil's novel takes two divergent paths: we are left with fragments unequally developed and irreconcilable.

A first version: brother and sister yield to their love, stateless refugees on an Adriatic island. Musil's notes, for a chapter entitled "The Journey to Paradise":

"It is our destiny: perhaps we love what is forbidden. But we will not kill ourselves before having made an ultimate attempt. The world is fleeting, fluid: do what you will. . . . A man never goes so far as when he doesn't know where he's going. . . ." They were standing now on a high balcony, intertwined and embracing the unspeakable like two lovers who, the next moment, will fling themselves into the void. They flung themselves. And the void bore them up. The moment remained motionless, neither rising nor sinking. Agathe and Ulrich experienced a felicity they could not distinguish from sadness; only the conviction of being chosen to live the exceptional restrained their tears. . . . With the limiting forms had vanished all limits, and since they no longer perceived any separation, neither in themselves nor in things, they no longer formed anything but a single being.

But this fulfillment on the island, symbolic of the abolition of the social, betrays the fundamental failure of all passion. "Between two isolated beings, there is no love possible," Ulrich admits. "A love can be born out of defiance; it cannot consist of defiance. It must be integrated into a society. It is not a content of life, but a negation, an exception opposed to all the possible contents of life. Now an exception must have something to which it is the exception. One cannot live on pure negation."

In an intellectualized form—these are simple *notes* for a sequel to be written—Musil here transposes the episode of the legendary lovers banished into the Forest of Morrois: the philter having ceased to act after three years, they discover that the world still exists and calls to them.

> *Dex! dist Tristan, quel departie!*
> (God, quoth Tristan, What misery!)

But there is more. Musil's lucidity here attacks the very formula of the Romance and destroys it. If passion does not lead to death, if the Day can reassert its rights, the experiment of forbidden love founders on reality, and the Romance in the most banal and depressing psychological analysis.

This is why Musil seems to have discarded this conclusion, which conforms with the logic of the Myth, in order to take the difficult path of a quest for mystical love: this is what he calls the "Millennial Kingdom" or the accession to the "other life," to the *state* of pure love, to the ecstasy of a love no longer egocentric, but allocentric: "No longer to have any center at all, to participate in the world without reservation, without keeping anything for the self; to cease, simply, to be." This attitude, which parallels Buddhist detachment but which could also manifest the redemption of passion by true love, is described in the magnificent chapter called "Breezes of a Summer Day." Here nothing occurs except a long conversation between the brother and the sister who love each other, in their garden where a silent snow of blossoms endlessly falls from the treetops onto the dark-green lawn.

At this point, passion gives way to presence, the suffering of desire to mutual ecstasy—but also the novel to the poem. A few moments before his death, Musil was working on this chapter, which would have been, some say, the conclusion of his work. Thus the *hortus clausus* of mystical presence would have replaced the island of mortal passion. And the "Journey to Paradise" of the earlier draft had become the "Journey to God" to which several notes for the book allude.

At the end of a novelistic periplus in which all the constant themes of passion have appeared and been developed one after the other, fading afterwards like islands passed on a voyage, this *hortus clausus* would be the Ithaca of a modern spiritual Odyssey. But doesn't this blissful presence in shared love also suggest a more intimate mystery, another redemption of Eros by Agapè? Mightn't the fascinating prohibition of love between brother and sister have been the disguise—quite unconscious, I'm convinced—of a love too real to dare speak its name *in a novel?* Happy love has no history, as everyone knows since novels were first written—novels that arouse passionate interest. But isn't this literary convention, condemning the fulfilled marriage, a taboo quite differently fearful, for both writer and reader, from any sort of incest or blasted passion? The eroticism of marriage is a *terra incognita* for Western literature. Perhaps Musil has unwittingly approached it closer than anyone else. I suggest for tomorrow's genius this remarkable precursor, whom lucidity alone has kept from finishing one of the most beautiful novels of yesterday's Europe.

IV

THE PASSION OF BORIS PASTERNAK

Results of a recent poll of the American public indicate that the majority of readers prefer novels written by a woman in the first person, describing everyday situations and normal emotions "that everyone has experienced or might experience," avoiding exoticism, praising the American way of life, and confirming its optimistic morality. If these were the tastes of the public, then these, according to the poll, would be the conditions required for a successful sale. At the same time, two novels were published in New York, both written by foreigners, Russians in fact; one described Revolutionary situations, the other emotions and obsessions which very few men and still fewer women can have experienced in the United States; one cruelly mocked the American way of life, the other was completely unaware of it; both ended in tragic failure, and implicitly condemned the society that crushed the central character. Yet these two novels disputed first place on the American best-seller lists for months on end.

Moreover it may seem that this sudden popularity (reducing the expert prognostications to nothing) is the only feature the two works share: it seems to me all the more surprising. I can see that one might attribute it to various accessory causes: moral scandal in the case of *Lolita*, political manifestation in that of *Doctor Zhivago*. But this doesn't explain everything, even if it is true, which I doubt.

Why is the poll silent about what for centuries (since, precisely, the twelfth century) has made the novel what it is (a *roman*, a romance), and makes us passionate readers? The public's preferences, if we credit the poll, should make the fortune of an American version of "socialist realism," from which love-as-passion is excluded. Yet what triumphs among this very public is two novels of love-as-passion. Shall we assume that it is a case of mass repression? Or simply that the questions asked suggested answers that conformed to the prejudices of the magazine taking the poll? What is certain is that love-as-passion continues to be regarded askance by, but fascinates, twentieth-century American men and women all the more, despite the progress of sexual education and

66

the rational preparation for marriage starting in grammar school.

Nonetheless, the awarding of the Nobel Prize having made *Doctor Zhivago* the object of a world-wide polemic in which the U.S.S.R. and the West confront each other once again—for reasons, moreover, that are not in this book—more than one reader will be sincerely shocked to find me speaking of it as a novel of love. Actually, my contention goes further: it is the *affaire Pasternak* in its entirety—I mean the drama between the author, the Russian people, and the regime, a drama prefigured in the novel itself—which I interpret as a case of love-as-passion. Let us consider the facts.

Pasternak writes a huge novel (of which only a portion will be published) describing the prodromes of the Russian Revolution, then the struggles of the heroic years up to the N.E.P., all without asserting the virtues of the Reds against the vices of the Whites. It is natural that the regime, being what it is, should condemn this book. It is natural that the condemned novel should manage to find its way to Europe, and be published. It is natural that the Nobel Prize jury should select it because it is a superb book and because its author has remained a free man. It is natural that the U.S.S.R., instead of interpreting this gesture as a kind of homage paid to its liberalism, should regard it as an offense to its authority. Natural, finally, that the Soviet writers' union should disguise its jealousy as loyalty to the regime and reject its celebrated colleague, covering him with official abuse.

In the world-wide uproar that ensued—homage in the West, outrage in the U.S.S.R. and letters from Zaporogue Cossacks to the Kremlin—everything is scandalously natural, up to this point.

But here is the extraordinary thing: when the Soviet authorities announce that they will not stand in the way of the writer's departure—which suggested a forthcoming decree of expulsion—Boris Pasternak sends the Master of Russia a pathetic letter whose importance lies in these two sentences: "Crossing the frontiers of my country would be equivalent to death for me, and that is why I beg you not to take this extreme measure in my regard. . . . I insist, my hand on my heart, that I have contributed to Soviet literature and that I can still be useful to it." He has refused the Prize, he is ready to forswear what is inimical to the regime in his book, provided he is left in communion with his people.

How are we to understand this step, taken by a man who cannot be suspected of cowardice? The Russian people condemns Pasternak for having spoken badly of the commissars. But Pasternak attacked the commissars for having betrayed the Russian people. If he now commends them in order to be restored to public favor, is it not Pasternak who betrays the people? This would indeed be the case if *Doctor Zhivago* were a political act, as many have chosen to believe on either side of the iron curtain.

Aware of the concealed presence of a logic entirely different from that which normally dictates political position and action, but having read only the first hundred pages of the novel when the crisis burst upon the world, I told myself: "Everything is happening as if this man were kept in his country by a secret and no doubt forbidden passion, as if he preferred anything, even forswearing his own work, to being separated from the object of his love, even if he has to live with it in humiliated and hopeless silence. But what can be the nature of this inaccessible Iseult, whose Tristan he seems to be? And who is the King Mark that separates him from her?"

I went on reading.

A young girl, Lara, wakens the nostalgia of Doctor Zhivago, whom she is nursing in a hospital, but she marries a revolutionary and vanishes. Zhivago finds her again much later. They declare their love for each other. Clandestine liaison. Again they are separated by the vicissitudes of the civil war. At last, chance reunites them in an abandoned house deep in the woods where Zhivago is hiding, pursued by the new police of a regime he has nonetheless served. They are offered a clandestine means of leaving Russia: Zhivago refuses. Lara is taken away from him by a powerful politician who had seduced her when she was still "a gamine." The doctor manages to get back to Moscow, where he lives in poverty and concealment. He marries, though he does not love, a young girl who takes care of his household, then leaves her and dies in the crowd. Inexplicably reappearing at this moment, Lara comes to mourn over his corpse. She is arrested soon after, and will die in Siberia.

Thus all the moments of the Legend are in evidence and recompose themselves, one after the other, with a mysterious exactitude. Iseult the healer, the remote nostalgia, the clandestine, forbidden mistress reft from Tristan by the man who symbolizes the ruling power—the flight into the forest, the second marriage, the last reunion of the lovers in death. There is only one novel in our literatures! Only one passion dictating the same vicissitudes ever since Tristan, ever since the great and decisive epiphany of passion's archetype, in the twelfth century.

Listen to it, this *alte Weise* renewed from Wagner's *Tristan.* Zhivago is talking to Lara in their forest retreat:

"Let us say farewell to our hopes, let us say farewell to each other. Let us tell each other once again our secret words of the night which is great and pacific, like the name of the Asian Ocean. It is not an accident you are here, my secret angel, *my forbidden angel,* under a sky of wars and insurrections; long ago, at the beginning of my life, under the calm sky of my childhood, you appeared in the same way. . . . Often, later, in the course of my life, I have tried to define, to give a name to the *luminous spell* you had cast over my soul, to that ray of light which gradually darkened, to that music which faded, which has dissolved with my very existence, which has become the key to all the doors of the world, thanks to you."

Once again, passion cuts off the world: Zhivago and Lara detest "the principles of a mendacious cult of society, transformed into politics." Once again, passion reveals itself first as a protest against society: "Even more than their community of soul, the abyss that separated them from the world united them. Both had the same aversion for all that is fatally typical of modern man, his ready-made enthusiasm, his bombast. . . . They were an exception . . . the breath of passion lay upon their condemned existence. . . ."

But who is Lara? In losing her, Zhivago says, "he would lose his reason for living and perhaps even life itself." Romantic exaggeration? No, it is a poet's vital truth. "From childhood, he loved the forest when at evening it was pierced by the light of the setting sun," and the decisive scenes of this poet's novel are always lit by the same red sun emerging beneath the clouds and penetrating the forest with its last rays. It is this image which shows him "in nature, in the setting sun, in all the visible world the enormous and innocent face of a little girl."

But here is the decisive admission; and the ambiguity which arrested me (are these novelists really talking about a society, an inner landscape, or a woman?) dissolves in a lyrical identity:

As a matter of fact, what was she for him? Oh! for this question he always had an answer ready.

It is a spring evening. The air is speckled with noises. The voices of children playing are everywhere, as though to show that space is vibrant with life. And that far horizon is Russia, that glorious incomparable mother whose fame stretches beyond the seas, that stubborn, extravagant, exalted, adored martyr with her ever-unforeseeable, forever sublime and tragic outbursts! Oh, how sweet it is to be alive! How sweet it is to live on earth and to love life! Oh, how one would like to thank life itself, existence itself, to thank them, and to their face. *Yes, Lara is all that.* Since one cannot communicate by words with these hidden forces, Lara is their representative, their symbol. She is both the sense of hearing and the words offered as a gift to the mute principles of existence.

From this moment, from this avowal, once the identity of Lara and Russia is explicitly stated, everything that has just occurred in the life of Boris Pasternak becomes clear. His letter to the Master of the Kremlin supplies us the terms anticipated in the scene where Komarovski (the adventurer who has been able to turn the Revolutionary government to his own advantage and who is to take Lara away) offers Zhivago exile. Without explaining his refusal, Zhivago answers: "There can be no question of my leaving." But later he adds:

> "Everything is already in your hands. It is likely that some day, exhausted, I shall have to swallow my pride and my self-esteem and humbly drag myself to your feet in order to receive from your hands Lara, life, the means of finding my family again, salvation. . . . Your news astounds me. I am crushed by a suffering that deprives me of all capacity to judge. . . . The only thing I can do now is to agree with you mechanically and to confide myself to you blindly. Hence, for Lara's sake, I am going to act a part. . . ."

V

PASSION AND SOCIETY

All passion feeds on negation, since it assumes and suffers *exception*, in the Kierkegaardian sense of the term. It exiles its victim. It destines this victim to contest with every breath everything that officially regulates social life. Hence the continual presence, in our three Tristanian novels, of society and its conventions; hence the mordant criticism to which the hero subjects them, speaking for the author: this criticism is part of the justification of passion, much more than a result of a different political or social system; in other words, the hostility of passion's victim is turned against the social in himself, and not provoked by the particular nature of the political regime in power. Thus Tristan, a model knight, is obliged to violate the feudal oath, becomes a traitor and felon, and finds himself exiled from the community of the gallant, not because he espouses some new doctrine heralding social subversions—of which there was no lack in the twelfth century—but because he has become the prey of a much more absolute power: *the state of passion.*

In *Love in the Western World* I have shown how this state precedes any specific object, how it creates its ideal object before identifying it with some real being by an essentially inevitable error which is then attributed to destiny. (My quotations from Musil have illustrated this point.) It is the state of passion which is loved first, in itself, rather than the inaccessible Iseult.

This state, in which true lovers, poets, mystics, and creators desire to remain once they have experienced it, while recognizing that they cannot survive in it, is described by all of them as indescribable. Sometimes it plunges those who suffer it into plaintive silence, some-

73

times it excites them to an inexhaustible loquacity—love letters, mystical treatises—that generally proceeds by antitheses and paradoxes. For there will never be enough words and metaphors and reinvented clichés and interlacing symbols to fix this indescribable reality that one tries so futilely to communicate. Hence the most common form of passion, since it is the most nearly communicable, is that which inspires the writing of novels, that whose contagion, rarely mortal but delicious, strikes all who have sensed, one day or another, the difference between a sexual desire and a state of the soul, the state of *being* in love. Amorous passion is, above all others, the one that lends itself best to narrative. Pure sexuality and love for one's neighbor are real only in action, and their description is soon tedious. The passion of Eros is true first in dreams, and perhaps never exists better than in the lyric impulse of its narration.

Bound so closely to literature by a complicity of both origin and essence, passion, as we have seen, is nonetheless dependent on the very society it denies: it is that society which has provided it, down to our own day, with the indispensable obstacles. On this point, two further observations.

It is remarkable that passion utilizes prohibitions and taboos only at the moment they begin to weaken, when it is still scandalous to violate them but does not involve an instantaneous repudiation, either physical or social, of the transgressor. The sexual freedom of young people in contemporary America, certain literary fashions of the

74

turn of the century, permit a Nabokov, a Musil to take their novels to the dangerous point where the scandal remains effective while the censor hesitates. The Romance of Tristan appears in history only when the Gregorian reform and the abuses it opposed had just aroused against the matrimonial laws not only the heresy of the South but the cultural elite of Europe. Hence Pasternak's novel appeared only after the Soviet "thaw": nothing is *won* as yet, but individuals can already admit something under cover of the Myth. Such is the biological "terrain" where the novel finds the best opportunities both to declare itself and to propagate its contagion.

There is more. The nature of the social prohibitions determines the psychological level and the very style of a novel. *Doctor Zhivago*, for instance, is by far the most traditional of the three novels just considered. Musil's work, on the contrary, exhibits so many formal, intellectual, and even mystical refinements that it ultimately escapes the *novelistic* altogether and suggests a new genre which might integrate into literature the most recent procedures of science and psychology. This is because the *nature of the obstacles* differs entirely in the two cases. Political and social in the U.S.S.R., hence external and, in a sense, more primitive, it does not call into play the same resources as in a more liberal or lax or decadent society: here, the obstacle is internalized, action becomes introspection, and plot a spiritual adventure.

Is this process irreversible? Does it herald the end of a genre, which would also be the end of this form of pas-

sion whose cult literature has maintained? What surviving taboos could still provoke the novelistic epiphanies of
Tristan and of love-as-passion?

Soviet totalitarianism and the conformism of mores
in the Western democracies are no longer defended
without scruples by elite circles on either side. I can see
no other prohibitions that are truly formidable, in the
eyes of twentieth-century man, but those which science
and hygiene might influence the State to enforce. The
passion that would violate them would no longer be condemned, but merely cared for, at the expense of Social
Security. What genius could counteract this plan of spiritual asepsis?

But I sometimes imagine other obstacles, more subtle
and tenacious than social taboos. I referred to them apropos of Musil. If it is true that passion seeks the Inaccessible, and if it is true that the Other as such remains the
best-defended mystery in the eyes of a demanding love
—could Eros and Agapè not join in a paradoxical alliance
at the very heart of accepted marriage? Is not every
Other the Inaccessible, and any woman loved an Iseult,
even if no moral prohibition, no taboo symbolizes (for
the requirements of the fable and the convenience of the
novelist) the very essence of the exciting obstacle, the
obstacle that will never depend on anything but being itself: the autonomy of the person loved, her fascinating
otherness?

76

TWO DANISH PRINCES
KIERKEGAARD AND HAMLET

In a dozen or so years, the career of Sören Kierkegaard unfolded as an intense, unified drama, inexorably motivated at every moment of its progress. His first important work, *Either/Or*, was published in 1843, when he was thirty, and achieved an enormous success. But as his message grew clearer, in a series of works written and published at the feverish rate of three or four volumes a year, the public turned away, appalled. And when in 1854 he directly attacked official Christendom and its bishops, who had praised his first works, he found himself ostracized, abandoned to the completest solitude a great mind has ever known. A year later, exhausted by his lonely duel against public opinion, he collapsed in the street during a walk. He was taken to a hospital, where he died in a few weeks at the age of forty-two.

The only external event of this drama was the breaking of his engagement with Regine Olsen, an initial crisis that released the spate of his entire *œuvre*. But the act which this *œuvre* was preparing, the act after which, like Prince Hamlet, that other Dane, he could die, certain of having fulfilled his mission, was his attack against modern Christendom in the name of Christ of the Gospels.

All his aesthetic and philosophical works appeared under various symbolic pseudonyms. He characterized these works as "indirect communications"; and these pseudonyms represented a *dramatis personae* to which he alone had the key. It was only at the end of his life that he advanced into battle without a mask, during the crucial polemic that was to lead him to his death.

Thus Kierkegaard's drama is typically that of a vocation. Its whole plot consists in the *gradual revelation* of the meaning and purpose of that vocation, secretly oriented, from the start, toward a single and startling action, for which the hero prepares himself at length, hesitating, drawing back, until an apparently minor incident provokes the final leap, the fulfillment, for which the hero pays with his life.

Now there exists, in Western literature, a prototype of this tragic action, a famous play whose form and progress suggest the most striking analogies with Kierkegaard's biography.

Without lingering over the attractive coincidence that makes Hamlet a Danish prince, let us first review the most salient features of the drama *invented* by Shakespeare, those which at first sight call to mind the drama *lived* by Kierkegaard and afford a possible parallel.

The story of *Hamlet* can be summarized as follows: a profoundly melancholy young man receives a terrifying mission, which he long hesitates to accept. This mission, which he can reveal only indirectly, isolates him from those around him, forces him to break off his engagement with the young Ophelia, and makes him pass for a dangerous lunatic. Finally, circumstances oblige him to execute the one act over which he wavers. He kills the usurper and perishes in this combat.

Profound melancholy, a secret that must be kept yet revealed, the breaking off of an engagement, and finally the open denunciation of a usurpation which all agree to pass over in silence: would not this summary of *Hamlet* serve just as well as a précis of Kierkegaard's biography?

Perhaps we can extend this parallel much further in its details, thereby illustrating both Kierkegaard's thought and life, and in a general way what might be called the laws or the psychology of a vocation.

Let us first consider the *character* of the two heroes, one imaginary, the other real.

Hamlet, a young prince, is an intellectual. His chief desire is to return to the University of Wittenberg and devote himself to philosophy. If he remains at court, it is only out of obedience to his mother's wishes. He cannot accept his share of the common human condition. An incurable melancholy possesses him, and he finds the uses of this world "weary, stale, flat, and unprofitable." He is tempted by suicide. But he manages to conceal this melancholy under a mask of sarcastic gaiety, a mordant wit given to irony and baroque metaphors. Now consider the terms Kierkegaard uses to describe himself. He too feels he is a prince. "There is something royal in my being," says one of his pseudonyms. He too would like to "return to Wittenberg," *i.e.*, devote himself to his dialectical genius, to the poetic and philosophical projects he had conceived while attending the Academy of Berlin; but he agrees to take nothing more than a degree in theology, out of obedience to his father's wishes. And above all, he too knows he is the victim of a kind of neurasthenia: "I have spent my youth in the grip of a tremendous melancholy, whose depths are equaled only by my faculty for concealing them under the appearance of gaiety." Or again: "I was armed with an almost reckless faith in my capacity to achieve all things, save one: to become free as a bird, even for a single day, to break the chains of melancholy in which another power confined me." This tendency, he adds, has condemned him to observe, to reflect life, to imitate rather than to live it in actuality; but though a prisoner of his agony, he has received "unlimited freedom to deceive."

Here then is Hamlet as the first scenes of Shakespeare's play describe him, and Kierkegaard as he reveals himself in his first work, *Either/Or:* two princes, two exceptional beings, full of boldness and pride, but alienated from ordinary life by a mysterious melancholy concealed beneath an ironic mask.

And it is just these two individuals, for whom life itself is already a problem, who further receive a fearful mission condemning them, even more than their psychological natures, to become exceptional beings.

Hamlet receives his mission from his father, who appears to him in the form of a ghost. Murdered, he claims, by the present king, who is thus no more than a usurper, the father commands his son to avenge him. Hamlet returns to his companions, who have watched the scene from a distance, and makes them swear three times to keep what they have seen a secret.

Kierkegaard too received in his youth the communication of a *secret*, to which he often refers, but whose nature he has never explained. We know, however, that the secret was linked to the memory of his father. He characterizes this revelation as the "great earthquake" in his life. It is in such terms that Hamlet might speak of his encounter with his father's ghost. And further, it was his father's influence that opened Kierkegaard's eyes to the *absolute* of true Christianity and brought him to this terrible knowledge: the self-styled Christianity of modern times is a cheat, an enormous illusion. "It resembles that of the New Testament no more than the *petit bourgeois* salon or the children's playroom resembles the most terrible choice of the cruelest reality." We have denatured Christianity, held it cheap, instead of recognizing ourselves as unworthy of it and admitting that we refuse to pay its price. This, Kierkegaard says, is "a crime of *lèse-majesté*." In other words, *usurpation*. Official Christendom plays in Kierkegaard's eyes the same role King Claudius plays in Hamlet's; only, while King Claudius had seduced the Queen, it is the Church which is abused by the edulcorated doctrine that people take for Christianity today.

Hamlet now knows his mission and his act: to kill the usurper, in order to re-establish legitimacy. And Kierkegaard realizes his vocation, which will be to denounce the religious usurpation in order to re-establish, in its original purity, the absolute exaction of the Gospels.

The task appears superhuman. And we find both heroes groaning under the burden that has been imposed upon them: "The time is out of joint; O cursed spite, that ever I was born to set it right!" Hamlet exclaims. And

Kierkegaard keeps ringing changes on the same idea: he was born to force our disordered age to recognize the Christian absolute and if not to obey it at least to cease calling itself Christian "cheaply." Both believe that "something is rotten in the state of Denmark," and that it will be their destiny to denounce this situation, come what may.

The characters given, the mission defined at the drama's start, let us now consider the progress of the action.

We must first take note of the role the *secret* plays in both cases. For Hamlet, it is quite simple: he must keep silent, or Claudius will certainly have him assassinated. For Kierkegaard, it is more complex: if he takes the offensive immediately, no one will listen to him. So he must begin by seducing the public, forcing it to pay attention to what he says, yet without betraying the real intent of his work. Kierkegaard lays his plans accordingly. He will first publish certain aesthetic works—brilliant, paradoxical, apparently cynical, and all under various pseudonyms. The Christian message, which is the only thing that matters to him, will be there, of course, but scrupulously concealed. In this way he will attract the public and lead it unwittingly to the most favorable point for his decisive attack. Now we recall that Hamlet lays an analogous plan. He arranges to have performed before the court a pantomime representing his father's murder and the usurpation of the throne. "The play's the thing," he says, "wherein I'll catch the conscience of the king." Both, then, choose indirect means—Hamlet actors, Kierkegaard pseudonyms—to turn interest, and at the same time arouse alarm, in the right direction, to suggest the secret without telling it, and finally to force the public or the court to "pay attention" despite themselves. (*Mundus vult decipi*, the world wants to be deceived, Kierkegaard remarks on several occasions.) But they have much to lose by such a stratagem. They risk creating the worst misunderstandings. And they also jeopardize their happiness. Here the parallel seems perfect.

Happiness, total participation in life, the sign of accession to the common human condition—for both men such things are represented by woman, love, and marriage. Yet both are constrained to renounce them on account of their mission, their secret—and perhaps too on account of their profoundly melancholy natures, and on this last point the doubt remains the same in both cases.

Kierkegaard has explained the breaking of his engagement with Regine. One might say he has explained it in his entire *œuvre*, and not only in works like "Guilty/Not Guilty" (in *Stages on Life's Way*), which are actually thinly disguised accounts of his engagement and the endless analysis of the motives for its collapse. Shakespeare, on the contrary, scarcely motivates Hamlet's attitude toward Ophelia at all. Here it is Kierkegaard's lived example that helps us to understand Hamlet.

Kierkegaard loves Regine, a girl of seventeen, and is loved by her. But he has his ambiguous secret, the secret of his vocation and that of his melancholy. He soon realizes that the secret would be too great a burden for the girl. Naive and spontaneous, she would simply try, if he revealed it to her, to bring her fiancé around to a more bourgeois view of existence and of religion. She would undermine his courage, depress his resolve, and become the worst inner obstacle to the exercise of his strange vocation. "Can a man marry if he wants to be a witness to the truth? Should a soldier at the frontier marry?" Kierkegaard asks himself. Then what about himself, fighting as he is at the outposts, the frontiers of the mind? Further, he fears initiating his fiancée into the "slavery of melancholy": he does not feel entitled to disturb this child, to expose her to torments to which he himself risks succumbing. "Who can understand," he writes, "this contradiction of suffering: not to reveal itself and cause love to die; to reveal itself and cause the beloved to die?" If he chooses to be the victim, only one path remains open to him: to break off with the girl he loves, but without letting her suspect for a moment the nature of his double secret; and therefore to convince his fiancée he no longer loves her. We *know* the farce Kierkegaard forces himself to act for Regine. He paints himself in her eyes as a kind of roué, a cynical seducer who may have serious misdeeds on his conscience and who renounces marriage in order to leave his bachelor delights unthreatened. He makes dreadful remarks at the moment of their separation: "She asked me: 'Then don't you ever want to marry?' I answered: 'Yes, in ten years, when the fire of youth has gone out: I'll need fresh blood to rejuvenate me.'" And Kierkegaard adds, as a commentary to this account: "Necessary cruelty!" He leaves her with simulated coldness, then runs off to the theater and, when he returns to his lodgings, cries all night. "But the next day," he writes, "I behaved as usual, and was even wittier than ever: it was necessary."

It seems to me that this behavior, in its duplicity that is more painful than scandalous, affords certain exact analogies with Hamlet's behavior toward that other child, Ophelia. Hamlet, too, has realized that Ophelia's naive and spontaneous love would constitute an obstacle to his secret designs. It is of Hamlet Kierkegaard was thinking when he wrote these lines, attributed moreover to a quite theoretical hero he has created: "I see that the notion of my existence founders on this young girl, *ergo* the young girl must vanish. My route toward a great goal passes over her ruin." And Hamlet, like Kierkegaard, denigrates himself in the young girl's eyes, claiming he doesn't love her, making the most cynical remarks, then exclaiming: "What should a man do but be merry?" Yet he admits in a later aside: "I must be cruel, only to be kind."

It is only fair to note here one profound difference between Kierkegaard and Hamlet: the former has done everything to keep Regine from suffering, has attempted to take all the drama upon himself, and believes he has succeeded in doing so, since he can write, not without bitterness: "She has chosen the crying, I have kept the pain"; while Hamlet drives Ophelia to suicide and seems indifferent to this disaster.

But let us come to the drama's denouement. A trivial incident sets off the catastrophe in *Hamlet*: a bout of foils. But Laertes' foil is poisoned: the duel for sport turns into a duel to the death. Wounded, Hamlet can no longer hesitate. He kills the king.

What, in Kierkegaard's case, is the equivalent of this climax in the drama, or of this tragic "fall"? A trivial incident, a simple phrase, and one that might pass for a cliché in any official address.

Bishop Mynster, Primate of the Danish Church, had just died. And Professor Martensen, in his funeral oration, felt obliged to salute his memory as that of a "genuine witness to the truth."

The poison, for Kierkegaard, was in this phrase. For his entire *œuvre*, his entire career as an author had had no other meaning, in his own eyes, than to re-establish in all its apostolic purity the concept of a witness to the truth, in other words, virtually the concept of a martyr. Now Bishop Mynster had been a great prelate, covered with titles and honors, a humanist of profound culture, a man rich in the goods of this world. To call him a witness to the truth was to commit toward the Christian absolute the crime of *lèse-majesté*, was to mock the Gospels, was to recognize and sanction the usurpation.

Kierkegaard felt he had been provoked. And here, too, what might have remained a simple bout of foils, a polemic like any other, suddenly turned into a duel to the death. Kierkegaard immediately wrote an article of extreme violence. He waited several months before publishing it—he waited until Professor Martensen had become bishop in his turn, succeeding Mynster. Then he published the article. And this article was his act, the direct act, decisive and mortal, as "exaggerated" as the lunge of a duelist who risks his life on a single thrust. Here is an extract from this article:

> A witness to the truth is a man whose life from beginning to end is familiar with every kind of suffering— with inner distress, with fear and trembling, doubts, scruples, anguish of the soul, torment of the mind, and further, all the sufferings people generally talk about in society. A witness to the truth is a man who bears witness in destitution, in poverty, in disgrace and humiliation, a man despised, detested, insulted, outraged, flouted; a man who is beaten, tortured, dragged from prison to prison, and then at last—for it is of a genuine witness to the truth that Professor Martensen speaks—and then at last crucified, decapitated, burnt at the stake, or roasted on a grille, and thrown on the trash heap by the executioner, without burial.
>
> That is a witness to the truth, his life and his existence, his death and his burial—and Bishop Mynster, says Professor Martensen, was one of the genuine witnesses to the truth.
>
> In truth, there is something more contrary to Christianity than any heresy or any schism—and that is to play at Christianity, to scamp its dangers and then to pretend that Bishop Mynster was a witness to the truth.

A furious controversy arose on all sides. Danish and Scandinavian public opinion was shaken with virtuous indignation. Kierkegaard fought alone against all comers. He launched a periodical pamphlet, *The Instant*, to broaden and intensify his offensive. After a year of battle, he succumbed.

He had dared the act; he had succeeded: the usurpa-

tion was denounced, and he had forced the public at
large to pay attention to his message. But instead of making himself a murderer, it was he who paid with his own
life. He became the martyr his work had called for.

Let us take note of that title: *The Instant.* Kierkegaard's thought had long been fascinated by the two
concepts of *the instant* and *the leap.* The instant, for him,
was the moment of faith, the contact of time and eternity, or, as he said, "the plenitude of time, when the eternal decision is realized in the partial occasion." The leap
was the movement proper to faith, irrational, instantaneous, concrete, that movement which the slightest doubt
could destroy, that pure risk on which one might founder but which, if not taken, left a man with nothing.[1]

Absorbed as I was in writing the preceding pages, and
in alternate readings of Kierkegaard and Shakespeare, I
confess that more than once I found myself uncertain
which of the two was speaking; it was easy to imagine
that *Hamlet* had been written by Kierkegaard, or else,
conversely, that the biography of Kierkegaard had been
put on the stage two and a half centuries before being
lived. Kierkegaard's "Elizabethan" style, his energetic
lyricism that mingles the trivial with poetic clichés, metaphors with puns, bursts of eloquence with dialectical pre-
ciosities—everything contributed to the illusion. Until

[1] This image of the leap reminds me of the final scene of Laurence
Olivier's splendid film of *Hamlet.* Hamlet, wounded, determined at
last to act, climbs onto a sort of raised tribunal and from there, with
a prodigious leap, flings himself out into space, sword brandished, to
fall upon the king, whom he kills. A perfect plastic translation of
Kierkegaard's favorite concepts.

the moment when I came across a note by Kierkegaard himself concerning *Hamlet*, which re-established the differences. Strangely, this two-page note is published as an appendix to the book in which Kierkegaard tells the drama of his betrothal. It would seem, then, that the parallel I have suggested occurred to Kierkegaard, and that he insisted on correcting it himself. Here is the substance of his note, entitled "An Oblique Glance at Shakespeare's Hamlet."

Kierkegaard reproaches Shakespeare for not having made *Hamlet* a religious drama. For if Hamlet's scruples are not of a religious order, the hero ceases to be genuinely tragic. He verges on the comic. If, on the contrary, his tergiversations derived from religious motives, they would become infinitely interesting, but there would no longer be a drama in the technical and aesthetic sense of the term.

Indeed, "in the aesthetic order, the obstacle must be external to the hero, not within him." If the obstacle to his act is within him, the question becomes one of religious scruples, and the hero is great only by his suffering, not by his triumph. There is no longer any exalting poetic *play*, there is only the serious, the existential. Let us translate this into other terms: if Hamlet were religious, there would be no *Hamlet* by Shakespeare, but merely Kierkegaard's biography.

Yet Kierkegaard's drama is not fictional. It has not been acted, and cannot be. It has been lived and suffered consciously (superconsciously, one might say), as the pure drama of a Christian vocation. Here ends, here "founders on existence" the parallel I have just drawn.

I have tried to illustrate, by means of images most familiar to us all, those of Shakespeare himself, certain mysterious moments in a completely inner dialectic. The risk of the undertaking is apparent: that of over-ingenuity. It is the technical risk, so to speak, of any "indirect communication." And now, out of loyalty to Kierkegaard's method, let us pass without transition to the "direct statement," to the examination of the nature or the mystery of a vocation experienced historically.

The first characteristic of a real vocation is its *ambiguity*.

This is immediately apparent in our current use of the term *vocation*. Hence one says of a young man that he has a vocation as a lawyer or a poet; this means he likes to argue or to make imaginative comparisons. Mozart, who composed minuets at the age of seven, no doubt had a musician's vocation. Here it is only the natural gift, the innate tendency, which is meant.

But there exists a quite different sense of the term. When the Lord commands Jeremiah to speak to the nations, he answers: "I cannot speak: for I am a child." We would say that he has no vocation. Precisely: he *receives* it. It is addressed to him despite what he is. "But the Lord said unto me, Say not, I am a child: for thou shalt go to all that I shall send thee, and whatsoever I command thee thou shalt speak. . . . Behold, I have put my words in thy mouth."

It is rarely possible to isolate from their context these

two contradictory movements: the impulsion of nature and the summons of the spirit. In Kierkegaard, the ambiguity subsists. We have noted that his profound melancholy separates him from others and, from childhood, makes his *nature* exceptional. But the religious call which he hears at the beginning of his writing career, and which charges him with a unique mission, makes him exceptional to a further degree, sets him apart a second time, for reasons which are those of the spirit—although, in this particular case, the nature and the call heard seem to push and pull in the same direction.

Hence this vocation could be interpreted in two quite contrary ways. One could say of Kierkegaard that he was neurasthenic, and that his case is one for psychoanalysis; or one could say that he was a prophet, born to be a poet and philosopher, but constrained by a transcendent imperative to become a witness to the truth.

Yet this ambiguity in our current sense of vocation is not the one which attracts Kierkegaard. He has distinguished another, more intimate ambiguity which no longer derives from the double sense of the word, but from the very existence of a *received* vocation.

The man, in fact, who receives a vocation finds himself hurled into an inevitable uncertainty by the call he believes he has heard. And his uncertainty is not the result of a lack of information, of a vague awareness or of a wavering will, but derives from the fact that there is no *proof* of the reality of the call nor of the reality of its object. In other words, as Kierkegaard says, the matter is one of an *objective uncertainty*.

Just as you cannot prove the existence of God, you cannot demonstrate the transcendent nature of a vocation. Of Jesus Christ one man will say: "He is a man called Jesus, the son of a carpenter from Nazareth," and another will confess: "He is the Christ, the Son of God, the Second Person of the Trinity." The objective uncertainty, as Kierkegaard defines it, is therefore a philosophic periphrasis to designate *faith* and its necessity. One can only "believe" in God, and one can only "believe" a vocation, whether it is another man's or one's own.

Hence the uncertainty is objective insofar as the object of one's conviction is not demonstrable; insofar, too, as the purpose of the vocation remains susceptible to doubt, or even denial; insofar as this purpose risks, after all, being purely imaginary.

To this should be added the *subjective* uncertainty, the uncertainty concerning the motives that might impel an individual to one thing or another: "Is this my secret nature or the spirit which has spoken?"

Thus the man with a vocation finds himself deep in a double uncertainty and in a permanent risk. There is no known method or line of reasoning that can help him. The man with a vocation commits himself by action and stakes all on something that remains as mysterious within as outside himself.

Let us return one last time to our dramatic parallel. We must admit, finally, that the mission received by Hamlet is not a true vocation, insofar as it does not offer the character of objective uncertainty implicit in every act of faith. Hamlet *knows* exactly what he should do: kill the usurper, avenge the murdered king. His goal is therefore unequivocal, his role clearly marked out in the general action. His uncertainty affects only the means to be used and, consequently, the final success. For Kierkegaard, for the Christian in general, matters proceed differently. It is a question of discovering the role we must play in an infinite drama as vast as human history, a drama whose course or movement no one can know—and yet we must act, we are in the world, we are on stage despite ourselves. Such is the anguish of vocation.

I pointed out earlier that Kierkegaard, in his earliest publications, had traced out a plan of action for himself involving a whole strategy of pseudonyms and "duplicities," as he keeps calling them. This would lead us to suppose that from his first appearance, like Hamlet, he had clearly seen the historical act he was charged to accomplish. But life is not so simple. It is generally *after the fact* that our actions appear to have been organized by a general intention. The intention, of course, functioned obscurely from the start, but it is only in action that we have sensed it at work. Kierkegaard realized this and expressed it in his work entitled "The Point of View for My Work as an Author":

> I must make a more precise reckoning of the share governance had in the authorship of my work. For in case I were to affirm out and out that from the very first I had a general view of the entire dialectical structure of my work, it would be a denial of God and dishonest toward him. . . . No, I must say truly that

what escapes me is that I can now understand the whole, and yet cannot by any means say that at the outset I understood it so precisely: and yet it is I who have carried it out and have made every step with reflection.

Were I now to express with the utmost categorical precision the share governance had in my whole activity as a writer, I know no more suggestive or decisive expression than this: it is governance that has educated me, and the education is reflected in the *processus* of my production. In view of this, it must be admitted that what I set forth above about my whole aesthetic production being a duplicity is not quite true, for such an expression assumes a little too much in the way of consciousness. At the same time, however, it is not altogether false, for I have been conscious of being under instruction, and that from the very first.

. . . The religious element is present from the very first instant and has a decisive predominance, but for a while it waits patiently to give the poet leave to talk himself out, though constantly on the watch with Argus eyes to make sure the poet does not fool it.

Finally, in the last pages of the book, he adds this: "All my work has been at the same time my own development: in it I have become conscious of my idea, of my task."

In another passage of the same book, he describes what might be called the psychology of a vocation in practice. He speaks of his total solitude. He describes himself not only as deprived of a confidant, but as alone with a self which even he no longer understands:

It would be futile for me to attempt to relate how I have sensed God's present aid. A thing has often happened to me, which I cannot explain: when I did something without knowing why or even thinking to ask why, when as a simple person I followed the prompting of my natural inclination, what had a purely personal significance, verging on the accidental, then proved to have an entirely different and purely ideal significance when it appeared later in my work; many things which I have done as a private individual turned out to be exactly what I should have done as an author. It was inexplicable to me that trivial and, as it seemed, accidental circumstances in my life (which, it must be said, were made to loom large by my imagination) brought on a certain mood; I did not understand, I became melancholy —when lo! there resulted from this precisely the mood I needed in relation to the work I was then occupied with, and at precisely the right place. . . . In a sense, I have produced my entire *œuvre* as if I had done nothing but copy out, every day, a definite portion of a book already printed.

Thus *vocation* organizes accidents and makes every stick an arrow, often without our knowing it. But what this passage best illustrates is the essential paradox of any vocation: one follows a path one thinks one is inventing, a path that remains invisible until one ventures to take it. The "light on my path" referred to in the Psalms does not illuminate a roadway marked out in advance far into the distance; no, the light is only "at my feet," it can reveal only the first step to be taken, and the path creates itself under the feet that tread it.

Here, the only human experience to which one can appeal by analogy seems to me to be the poetic experience. For the poet, too, does not and cannot ever know if he is merely submitting to an errant rhythm, or if he is actually creating—though apparently following—it.

To advance thus in life is virtually to live in the improbable, it is to be forever ready to confront the *absurd*. If objective uncertainty is the first characteristic of a real vocation, the acceptance of the absurd is its necessary consequence.

Kierkegaard keeps insisting on this last category: "He who does not renounce plausibility never enters into relation with God." If Abraham had not accepted the absurd, he would never have set out for a country about which he knew nothing. But we must understand that to accept the absurd is to renounce not only the common formulas of success, but all justification in public and even, in certain cases, public morality. It is to run an absolute risk.

What help, what landmarks, what directing principles, then, does Kierkegaard offer us? In truth, the only guide he suggests is suffering, when he writes this sentence charged with meaning: "It is not the way which is difficult, it is the difficult which is the way."

Here we see that Kierkegaard's concept of vocation is diametrically opposed to the currently accepted one. For in the word's present sense, to follow one's vocation is to move in the direction nature urges us, in the direction of our talents, our "facilities," while Kierkegaard proposes suffering not only as the sign and guarantee of the true way, but, more radically, as the way itself.

DON JUAN

WHEN HE STRIDES on stage, glittering in silk and gold, the heroic seducer at his proudest, we are tempted to see in him only the natural fire of desire, a kind of vehement and somehow innocent animality. But Nature has never produced anything like this.

We sense there is something demonic about him, almost a polemic of defiant wickedness: the hand extended to the Commendatore in the last act of Mozart's opera. Now this is not the animal but the man, and not prior to but after morality. There is no Don Juan among the "noble savages" or the "primitives" we hear about. Don Juan presupposes a society encumbered with exact rules which it prefers to infringe rather than throw off.

In the intoxication of anarchy he thrives on, this *grand seigneur* never forgets his rank. His natural mood is scorn; nothing is further from nature. Consider how he treats women: incapable of possessing them, he first violates them morally in order to subjugate the animal part of their being; and no sooner has he taken than he rejects them, as if he sought the fact of the crime rather than the gratifications of pleasure. A perpetual polemicist, he happens to be completely determined by the good and the just—against them. If the laws of morality did not exist, he would invent them in order to violate them. Which is what suggests to us the spiritual nature of his secret, so carefully masked by the pretext of instinct. On the summits of the mind in revolt, we shall see Nietzsche renew this mortal challenge a hundred years later.

But need we seek so far? Isn't the "perfectly natural" search for desire's intensity enough to explain this frenzy of inconstancy? Then Don Juan would be the man of the first encounter, of the most exciting victory. "Novelty is the tyrant of our soul," wrote the old Casanova. But it is already no longer the voluptuary who speaks thus. The true sensualist's joys lie beyond those moments Don Juan flees as soon as they are within his grasp.

Must we resort to the indiscreet doctors of the School of Vienna? A splendid opportunity for them, and one they have not missed. For them, too, Don Juan is the contrary of what we suppose; he suffers from a secret anxiety bordering on impotence. And it is true that the man who yields to that superficial attraction which almost every pretty woman can exert over almost every man does not suggest the image of health. But in this insolent fury, in this gay and querulous swagger, how can we see nothing more than weakness and deficiency?

Perhaps we might go further, applying spiritual criteria? For instance, Don Juan might be the type of man who does not achieve that personal level where what is unique in a human being can be manifested. Why can he desire only novelty in a woman? And why does he seek the new, something new at any price, whatever it may be? The man who seeks is the man who *has not*, but perhaps also the man who *is not*. The man who has, lives by his

possession and does not abandon it for the Uncertain—
that is, if he truly possesses. Don Juan might be the man
who cannot love, because loving is first of all choosing,
and to choose one must *be*, and Don Juan has no being.
But the contrary is no less likely: Don Juan seeking
everywhere his ideal, his "type" of female beauty (unconscious memory of his mother)—too quickly seduced
by the most fleeting resemblance, always disappointed
by the reality as soon as he approaches it, already dashing
off toward other appearances, ever more agonized and
cruel. What if he found his "type"! I can imagine the
metamorphosis. We see him stop short, suddenly change
expression, lower his head, grow somber, as though suddenly turning shy, and fascinated for the first time by
love's revelation, transform himself into the image of
Tristan.

But he will not find his type. He is Don Juan because
we know he cannot find it, either impotent to attach
himself, or impotent to release himself from an obsessive
image. Hence his apparent power, his *furia*, his dionysiac
rhythm.

Now if Don Juanism is a passion of the mind and not,
as we used to think, an instinctual exultation, everything
suggests that this passion is not *always* linked to sex. One
even wonders if sensuality, in fact, is not the very realm
in which Don Juan reveals himself as least dangerous.
(Let us here define danger as what can compromise a
certain social equilibrium which it is the purpose of manners to maintain, that equilibrium being, moreover, either good or bad.) This is because the desire for novelty

and perpetual change, once the insatiable mind provokes it, becomes a threat to life. In diverting this passion toward pleasure, society manages to afford it satisfactions which exhaust it, without endangering the established order by unproductive expenditures.

Of course Don Juan is a cheat—in fact that is how he lives (the faro table was Casanova's great financial resource: a symbol he explains many times over). But constant cheating is less dangerous than the sudden defections of an honest man. We are on guard, and we know the system, which is at every point related to the rules of the game. Let us imagine a more secret Don Juanism, a faro table where one puts invisible "values" on the cards instead of clinking coins. Then the cheating ceases to be a vulgar and profitable manipulation. It can become the heroic act of an honesty without scruples, still considered criminal because it institutes, with subversive rigor, a new order.

Nietzsche took his stand in opposition to the age. And the adversary he chose is the spirit of inertia, our natural weight, our natural faculty for falling back into habit. The immoralist, like the moralist, is a vigilant enemy of instinct: for if he glorifies it, it is in a polemical spirit; it is because he wants to assault nature in a new way.

He proceeds from challenge to challenge, first aroused then exasperated by the adversary's silence or cowardice. Ideas turn themselves inside out at the mind's whim: no truth can any longer endure. Men surrender or fall into doubt at the first blandishment of a scientific hypothesis.

No longer is there a faith which affirms and maintains by virtue of the absurd. How tired one grows of winning at every throw, merely by denying rules no one now dares call inviolable! Who would die these days for a virtue whose goal no one knows? And look how quickly all these venerable truths have yielded! Soon only God and his Son will be left. Already "the moral God is refuted." What will the Other One say? In the biography of the Don Juan of truths, this is the moment of the Commendatore's invitation! Yet God says nothing. He does not accept the challenge. Nietzsche waits, in the vacant night of the peaks. When dawn comes, it is only another earthly dawn. No one has spoken. God is dead!

Nietzsche wanted to *violate* the secret of each idea, of each belief, of each value; and their swift defeat renders them all contemptible after the first possession. Why should he linger over them? They were exciting for the mind only by the false virtue that was attributed to them. But once they have betrayed the vulgarity they have in common, victory loses all its savor. Now he must destroy the new values he had invented for the struggle. He must disgustedly reject what he had so impetuously desired, must turn the laugh on the followers, the successors, the disciples emboldened by another's glowing triumph, who already suppose they can abuse his victims.

Mille e tre truths have surrendered, and not one has been able to hold him.

What do "contradictions" matter! It is not in order to construct a system that he disputes, denounces, and destroys; it is for the joy of intellectual rape. As Don

Juan pursues the image of the Mother, Nietzsche pursues the obscure and obsessive image of a Truth that will not surrender but possess him forever, worthy at last of his true passion! He unrelentingly hunts down everything that moves, everything that stops, everything that appears to resist. Brief pleasures—the interval of an aphorism, a lightning flash that is always disappointing: it is not *she* whom he has just possessed. O hatred of their feeble truths! Truth is dead! Will she live again?

For if this God is dead forever, love is now impossible. He must *invent* a love which at least permits him to hate everything that fades, that yields, all the shamelessness and lethargy of the world.

It is at the point of dionysiac fury where joy in destruction turns to pain, and in the agony of a power annihilated by its own success, that Nietzsche suddenly encounters the fascinating idea of the Eternal Return. Confronting the Sils-Maria rock, we see him stop short, change expression, and for the first time lower his head and adore. Everything will eternally return to this moment, to this instant! Eternity is the return of time; and no longer the victory over time. But in time, he said, God has died. If God is dead, then he must have lived? God will live again, eternally! Thus Nietzsche becomes the Tristan of a destiny he can possess only by a love that is eternally *distant*.

A cheat, Don Juan makes love without loving. If he triumphs, it is by violating the truth of human beings. Nietzsche sets up values which destroy the old rules, but which are valid only because of these rules and insofar as they are felt to violate them. Should he succeed in imposing them, they would lose their meaning, since the system that measured them would no longer exist. Beyond good and evil, beyond the rules of the game, a passion must reveal itself; either death or eternal life. So Don Juan must vanish (for Don Juan won only by cheating, and if there are no longer any rules, one can no longer cheat).

Here perhaps is the key to the mystery: *in respecting all the rules, we could never do anything but lose.* Then: either we shall be damned, or else we shall receive our pardon. But Nietzsche and Don Juan do not believe in pardon, so they are either obliged to win during the time-span of their lives—hence the cheating; or else they must deny the end of time, the final reckoning, the last judgment—hence the notion of the Eternal Return.

As I was speaking of these things to a friend: "I used to know," she said, "a married man with whom I flirted to no purpose, and as we separated he said: 'I'm adding you to my list of the *mille e tre*.' They were the women he had not had, out of faithfulness to his own wife."

Where is the cheating here? In the challenge, instituted at the heart of the rule?

DIALECTIC OF THE MYTHS (I)

Meditation at the Fabulous Crossroads

In Gribs-Forest, there is a place called the Nook of Eight Paths: he alone finds it who worthily seeks it, for it is not indicated on any map. The very name seems to involve a contradiction. For how can the junction of eight paths constitute a nook? How can that which implies travel in all directions accord with what is lonely and concealed? And if what the solitary man shuns is named after the junction of only three paths: *triviality*—how trivial then must be the junction of eight paths! And yet it is so: there actually are eight paths, but very solitary paths. . . . Quite nearby, a grove set about with hedges is called the Fatal Close. . . . The eight paths, the quantity of traffic are merely a possibility, a possibility for thought, since no one frequents these paths except a tiny insect which hurries across them *lente festinans*. . . . No one frequents these paths except the wind of which no man knows whence it cometh and whither it goeth.

"In Vino Veritas"

KIERKEGAARD actually *lived* Tristan's unique love, his doomed passion, but his early pseudonymous books suggest the flight of a dark butterfly fascinated by the flame of Don Juan. Nietzsche lived still more to himself, and no less chastely, but his entire work leads the infernal dance of a "Don Juan of knowledge" until the day when he stops, "nailed" on the threshold of an Eternity in which he discovers his Isolde. For both, thought is a passion, and the total expression of passion can only be musical. "By music, the passions delight in themselves." [1] Both accede, one by Mozart and the other by Wagner, to the core of the myth which by themselves they could only dream of, which their persons refuse, and which is their Shadow.

I have long sought a perspective that might include these two destitute lives and at the same time these two inexhaustible *œuvres*; these two major myths of love and their perfect epiphanies in Western lyricism.

In the spiritual quest of a true vision, or perhaps merely of a felicitous and penetrating insight, one truly situating the man who sees as well as the object seen, we may sense the proximity of a significant halting place —the "Fatal Close" is not far off, but at the same time avenues lead away. Such crossroads, "not indicated on any map," are enthralling sites for a man seeking adventure deep in the forests of the Western soul.

Let us pause here to meditate. And then follow now this lane of light traced through the treetops by the oblique rays of the afternoon sun, now this darkened glade stirred by a sudden wind, of which no man knows whence it cometh and whither it goeth.

[1] Nietzsche, *Beyond Good and Evil*, § 106.

I

KIERKEGAARD AND DON JUAN

It is deep in the great forests of northern Zealand, one summer evening, that the guests of the banquet meet in front of a hunting lodge:

> The folding doors were thrown open; the sparkling illumination, the gusts of cool air, the seductive fragrance of perfume, the impeccable taste of the dinner service momentarily overwhelmed the guests who were on the point of entering the room, and when at the same instant the orchestra began playing the ballet music from *Don Giovanni*, they felt transfigured, and as though in stunned reverence before an invisible spirit, stopped for a moment in their tracks, like a man whom enthusiasm has stirred and who comes to himself in the midst of his enthusiasm.

This page introducing the speeches on love that compose "In Vino Veritas" gives the tone of Kierkegaard's passion for Mozart's *Don Giovanni*. In his Journal for 1839, we already find, apropos of Molière:

> In a sense I can say of Don Juan what Donna Elvira says to him: "Thou murderer of my happiness." For in truth: this play has so diabolically enraptured me that I can never forget it. It is this play that has driven me, like Elvira, out of the calm night of the cloister.

Ultimately it is thanks to Mozart, Kierkegaard writes later on—in *Either/Or*—that he has not lived without having loved, "though such love was doomed."

Linked by these last words to the solitary's all too real life, the fascination of the myth here reveals its true nature as existential virtuality. Kierkegaard's real life has defined itself by his rejection of the Don Juan myth, a permanent—and permanently abjured—temptation. This is why no one else has judged this myth so well.

Kierkegaard's interpretation of Don Juan rivals Mozart's in its magnificence: it reinvents the drama's structure as though by a creation of intrepid logic. It imposes on us, by virtue of an unforgettable coherence, a triple and unique interpretation of the opera, the myth, and the essence of Western music. Here is the argument, in condensed form.

Christianity, being spirit, has posited sensuality in the world. Because it excluded sensuality in principle, Christianity has posited it as a principle and as a spiritual category. Eroticism, a "psycho-sensual synthesis" determined by spirit, henceforth requires a language capable of translating its spontaneity. Only music can serve this function. For it is a language of the senses, but the sense of hearing, more than any other, is "determined by spirit." Music, further, is, next to speech, the least material medium of the idea: it exists only in time, in a succession of moments, then disappears, unlike plastic works, whether painted or sculptured.

Eroticism, excluded by spirit, will therefore find its "absolute medium" not in speech, but in music; and similarly music will find its "absolute object" in sensual genius, for "the sensual mood is too heavy and too dense to be sustained by speech; only music can express it."

If Don Juan represents pure desire in its irresistible and demoniac genius, "determined by spirit as being that which spirit excludes," the expression of Don Juan can only be musical. And this is why the only Don Juan that conforms to the myth[2] is Mozart's *Don Giovanni.*

Here is his description according to Kierkegaard. Don Juan is a power, and not a person:

> When Don Juan is conceived musically, I understand infinity within him, but also the infinite power of passion, which nothing can resist; I understand the frenzied possessiveness of desire, but also the absolute triumph of this desire, a triumph it would be pointless to oppose. If perchance thought lingers over the obstacle, the latter derives its importance from arousing passion rather than from actually opposing it; the pleasure is thereby increased, the victory is certain and the obstacle only a stimulant. I find in Don Juan a life thus animated by a powerful and irresistible demoniac strain, in the manner of an element. Such is his ideality in which I can delight with a tranquil mind, because the music does not represent him to me as a person or individual, but as a power.[3]

Don Juan is a movement, a pure tension—or nothing. Like a stone skipping along the surface of the water, he instantaneously sinks into the abyss after the last ricochet.

Irresponsible, like every natural force, Don Juan therefore incarnates, so to speak, absolute moral nihilism.

[2] Kierkegaard says in Hegelian terms: conforms to the pure idea, to ideality, to the aesthetic category. He has no difficulty proving that Molière's, Heiberg's, and Byron's Don Juans are far from the mark in this regard.

[3] *Either/Or,* "The Musical Erotic."

He seduces by the mere energy of desire. "I cannot imagine him formulating his plans in secret, carefully calculating the effect of his intrigues. . . . He never stops to think. . . . He requires no preparation, no plan, no time; for he is always prepared. His energy and desire are never-failing, and only when he desires is he in his proper element." He does not dazzle Zerlina with fine words, he invites her to come in, makes a gesture. "He does not seduce, but he desires, and this desire has a seductive effect."

"Not only does he enjoy success with women, but he makes them happy—and unhappy; but curiously enough, that is what they want, and they consider a girl foolish who would not choose to be unhappy for the sake of having once been happy with Don Juan." Don Juan is convinced that "the true expression of woman consists in her desire to be seduced. . . . This is why she never turns against her seducer, at least not if he has truly seduced her." [4]

---

[4] Casanova would conform much more closely to Kierkegaard's definition of the Don Juan type—if not to Mozart's!—than the Valmonts, Lovelaces, and other Machiavellian seducers of the eighteenth century, who leave only rage, shame, and contempt behind them. Casanova loves women; Valmont seeks only to win matches.

It is one of the commonplaces of modern criticism to deny Casanova's Don Juanesque character. Of course, Casanova is neither impious nor demonic, provokes neither God nor man. He is not revolutionary, nor is he a *grand seigneur*. He is a cheat, a vulgarian, a Catholic only when it suits him yet not an atheist, an occultist for show yet extremely superstitious. Finally, he is satisfied with easy conquests. (But what suggests that Don Juan disdains them? Certainly not the Catalogue!) So much, then, for the essentials. But Don Juan never existed, he is a myth; and the greatest difference between Casanova and the myth is that the *Mémoires* really exist. As for the historical points of contact between the Venetian and *Don Giovanni*,

Don Juan's eroticism is opposed to the ancient Eros, which was psychical, not sensual, "and it is this which inspires the modesty characterizing all Greek love." [5] It is opposed even more sharply to chivalrous love, which is essentially faithful. "Psychical love is a duration in time, sensual love a disappearance in time, hence the medium which exactly expresses it is music." For Don Juan, "an entirely abstract femininity is the essential thing," individuality does not exist: in his eyes, there will never be infidelity or deception, but only repetition and multiplicity. His life being only "a sum of distinct moments . . . a total of instants," Don Juan cannot have a biography: to provide him with a childhood and adolescence was Byron's fatal mistake. He is the genius of the moment. His conquests are without history, "for he has no time." "To see and love her are one and the same thing . . . and immediately everything is over, then repeated to infinity." Without past, without memory (he needs the Catalogue!), without future, and without nostalgia, he turns up, takes his pleasure, and takes off, until he collides with the "stumbling block," the stone statue of the Commendatore. But the Commendatore is a spirit! He is even a ghost, hence a return of the past. He represents the spiritual negation of the spon-

we need merely recall the friendship between Da Ponte and Casanova at the period when the Abbé wrote his libretto, the visit the two cronies made to Mozart at the time, Casanova's presence at the première of *Don Giovanni* in Prague, and lastly a variant of the Second Act sextet found among his papers at Dux.

[5] Compare Nietzsche: "The most modest remark I ever heard: *in true love, the soul contains the body.*" (*Beyond Good and Evil*, § 142.)

taneous genius of the moment. He alone, therefore, can overcome Don Juan, no power of *this* world having got the better of him.

Kierkegaard's account of the myth is not only inspired by Mozart: its goal is to demonstrate that Mozart's opera *is* the myth itself, integrally manifested in each detail as in the style and structure of the whole. Interpretations of the legend may have varied "until Mozart discovered both its true medium and its idea," whence "the absolute classic value" of his opera. Any number of *Fausts* [6] might be written, for "the idea of *Faust* supposes such maturity of mind that it is natural for there to be several conceptions of it," each one "perfect" for a generation; while Mozart's *Don Giovanni*, "by the abstract character of the idea, will live eternally and for all time." To write another after Mozart would be to produce an *Ilias post Homerum*.

From the commentary on the opera itself (whose strictly musical pertinence is staggering, though Kierkegaard calls himself an "amateur" without any technical competence), let us recall this central observation:

---

[6] Kierkegaard sees clearly the relationship of the Faust and Don Juan myths. (See in particular the essay on Marguerite in *Either/Or*, "Shadowgraphs.") In Mlle Micheline Sauvage's learned and intelligent work *Le Cas Don Juan* (a single, almost incredible, lacuna: Kierkegaard is not even mentioned), I find these skillfully balanced formulae: "Don Juan and Faust are mythic twins . . . complementary halves of a double being. . . . Don Juan is intelligent, lucid, he has a Faustian mind; Faust is voluptuous, eager for love, he has a Don Juanesque heart and senses. . . . Faust is the intelligence of Don Juan; Don Juan is Faust's eroticism. . . . Romanticism will conclude that Don Juan and Faust both seek the absolute, and that the same hero is called Faust when he pursues this absolute in knowledge, Don Juan when he pursues it in pleasure."

"Don Juan lends interest to all the other characters. . . .
His passion sets the passion of all the others in motion;
his passion echoes everywhere." Don Juan being not a
character, but a power and vitality, hence "absolutely
musical," the other characters, who are merely passions
determined by Don Juan, are musical to this very
degree. "One may come in at any point during the performance and instantly be in the center of it, because
this center, which is Don Juan's vitality, is everywhere."
The only character who seems an exception to this rule
is, naturally, the Commendatore, but in a sense (which
the analysis of the musical themes makes clear) he is
"placed outside the play, or circumscribes it." As time
is circumscribed by eternity.

II

KIERKEGAARD AND TRISTAN

Yet Kierkegaard was the opposite of a Don Juan. In
relation to his work, his public action, and his ultimate
vocation, he was Hamlet. But in his private life, in his
unique and doomed love for Regine, he was Tristan.
Yet in all his works I have found only rare allusions to
Shakespeare's *Hamlet* and not one reference to Tristan
—for hundreds of lyrical and enthusiastic pages on the
Don Juan of legend and of Mozart.

The contrast between this discretion, even this deliberate silence, and this verbal luxuriance is the kind
that expresses the essential characteristics of a person.

What does Don Juan mean to this bachelor who is perfectly free to lead his life as he pleases, rich and leisured, brilliant, interested in everything but also rather sickly ("*Give me a body!*" he groans in his Journal)? What is Don Juan to this solitary who anticipates his genius as a writer and his religious vocation? From all evidence, Don Juan is the image of himself that tempts him most: it is his *potential self*, glamorous, desired, but a self he cannot and will not make a reality. In abjuring it, he sees and defines that self superlatively; at the same time, he defines *himself*, against but not without that self. He conceives only two ways of living worthy of the absolute and possible for himself: either the *seducer* or the *recluse*.[7] Both exclude marriage, "love's supreme expression," which he has had to renounce for a reason which remains his last secret. Marriage abjured, if he decides to be an anchorite, the seducer becomes his *myth*. Don Juan becomes his shadow, though more brilliant than himself, and one he must ceaselessly exalt and condemn, for his shadow is himself as much as any other part of himself, but it is what he refuses in himself. It is what he *could* be, exemplarily, if he were not what he endures, suffers, and struggles to transcend in the direction of the absolute, in the direction of what he wants to become according to spirit.

If such is his myth, his virtual Eros, then what is the actual, historically experienced form of his Eros? It is passion—unique, total, and doomed passion; and by that very doom, redeeming.

[7] *Stages on Life's Way*, "Various Observations about Marriage."

Human love is based on an instinct which, raised to the order of inclination, finds its supreme, unique, and absolute (poetically absolute) expression in the fact that there is only one beloved being in the world, and that love's "once only" *is* love, and that the "second time" is nothing. . . . Once is the absolute, a second time is absolute ruin.[8]

Of course the Young Man of "In Vino Veritas," who has not yet loved, finds it easy to pillory the tragicomic absurdity of passion's unappealable choice, which is of crucial importance yet can only be made "blindly." How explain "so monstrous an act of selection"? Is not the passionate lover, in his exclusive choice, "a marionette whose strings are drawn by something inexplicable?" Such a point of view, replies Johannes the Seducer, merely proves that "our young friend remains outside," that is, as yet maintains only abstract relations with life, for "the resolution, the resolution of lust, is the point of life." One must choose in order to exist. The Seducer chooses to love as often as he can, for it is woman he loves, and in each real woman there is *that* which wants to be seduced and which can be seduced only once. On the other hand, the Husband—who will speak in the second part of the *Stages*—chooses to love one woman alone and to marry her, for marriage is that decision which "translates exaltation into reality." Far from impoverishing the experience of life, this decision alone can lead to it. It is the decision par excellence, which makes existence concrete. By it, married life becomes "the fullness of time"—that time which Don Juan never has.

[8] *The Works of Love*, 1847.

Still, the Husband does not mean to escape the fundamental difficulty of marriage, and even formulates it at
the start: "Love and amorous inclination are entirely
spontaneous, marriage is a decision; to want to marry
means that what is most spontaneous must at the same
time be the freest decision. . . . Further, one of these
things may not follow the other, the decision must not
be made stealthily from the rear: the whole thing must
occur simultaneously." There follow a hundred pages
in which the Husband reiterates by philosophical argument that the decision cannot be based on argumenta-
tion. It is not surprising that this work is unconvincing:
Kierkegaard is behind the pseudonyms, exalting a Don
Juan he rejects but who remains a *possibility;* he is not
behind the Husband. For the Husband represents and
defends the impossibility which Kierkegaard endures,
and which he will attempt to explain—to justify—in all
the rest of his work.

Let us grant that true love is a unique and shared
passion. To be happy, in marriage for example, this love
must perform the miracle of "making the different the
same," thereby creating the possibility of a true understanding. But this remains theoretical. It will be understood by the roundabout means of Kierkegaard's theology. In his religious works, he constantly comes back to
the "infinite qualitative difference between God and
man," which makes of the relations between man and
God a love doomed in essence. This love would actually
be impossible were it not for the paradox of faith, which
is a movement of passion, a leap. Any direct communica-

tion from God to man would kill man, that is, would kill his power of free and subjective appropriation of the truth. Hence it is divine love itself which requires the indirect, veiled communication that reaches man here where he exists, in his finitude, and speaks to him in the language he understands. But then the message becomes enigmatic precisely to the degree that it has been able to make itself perceptible.

What happens between Kierkegaard and his fiancée seems to derive from an analogous structure of possible and impossible communication. He loves her, she loves him, but the secret he bears (his "melancholy," as he says, but also the presentiment of his exceptional vocation) forbids him to enter with her into that rapport of direct, equalizing communication which he considers marriage to be. Out of love for Regine, he must therefore leave her, though he continues to address her, under cover of his pseudonyms, and to dedicate all his works to her as so many justifications for the breaking of the engagement and assurances of his faith. "Who will understand this contradiction of suffering: not to reveal oneself is the death of love; to reveal oneself is the death of the beloved?" [9]

To attempt to determine if Kierkegaard's theological attitude "explains" his amorous behavior, or if it is not rather the inverse that applies—would correspond to nothing in our perspective and would help to reveal no verifiable *meaning*. As a matter of fact, every thinking man possesses a system—more or less "original" but

[9] *Philosophical Fragments*, "God as Teacher and Savior."

always unique—of apprehending reality in all its forms. This system defines his individuality. Now I am here considering and attempting to grasp only a certain dynamic structure: Kierkegaard in his inseparable life and work; and I see that this structure is arranged in such a manner that the "aesthetic" and the "religious" are constantly homologous, both irrigated by passional energy, while the intermediary "ethical" stage seems spiritless, schematic, and unstructured. A single example: the decision on which marriage is based also symbolized, as we have seen, the very basis of every existential ethic. Yet this decision escapes man, hence escapes the temporal and autonomous ethic:

> The decision is not within men's power, courage, or skill . . . it is a religious point of departure; if it is not, he who decides has been made finite only in his reflection, he has not immediately adopted the amorous inclination, but has remained upon the way, and such a decision is so wretched that the amorous inclination scorns it, preferring to trust to itself rather than obey the dictates of such a false teacher. The spontaneity of amorous inclination recognizes only one spontaneity as being equal in rank to itself, and that is religious spontaneity.[10]

Hence, as Kierkegaard reiterates a little farther on, "the absurdity of amorous inclination reaches a divine understanding with the absurdity of religious feeling." But we realize that it never reaches such an understanding with a passionless morality.

I see, finally, that for Kierkegaard the person is that

[10] *Stages on Life's Way,* "Various Observations about Marriage."

system which defines itself by the tension and interdependence of three heterogeneous realities: his belief in the total otherness of God and in the one-sidedness of human love; the "melancholy" that overwhelms him and makes marriage impossible for him; finally, his exceptional vocation.

Marriage is forbidden to the man who must be the Exception:

> Is a soldier on guard at the frontier permitted to be married? Dare such a soldier (spiritually understood) take a wife, if he is fighting day and night not against Tartars and Scythians, but against the pirate hordes of an innate melancholy? [11]

Love is the privileged agent of the "superior man's" spiritual progress—always on condition that he not be "happy":

> Thanks to a young girl many men have become geniuses, many have become heroes, many poets, many saints—but not one was a genius by means of the young girl he possessed, for by her he became only a Councillor of State; not one was a hero by the girl he possessed, for by her he became only a general; not one was a poet by the young girl he possessed, for by her he became only a father; and not one was a saint by the young girl he possessed, for he possessed none, and wished to possess only one, whom he did not obtain, just as all the others became geniuses, heroes, poets thanks to the young girl they did not possess. If the ideality woman bears within her has awakened enthusiasm in a man, he should therefore have united himself for life with this woman who

[11] *Stages on Life's Way,* "Guilty/Not Guilty."

has thus roused his enthusiasm. But existence states the matter otherwise. Thus all this signifies that it is in a negative relation that woman renders man productive in ideality. Understood in this fashion, woman leads to the heights.

This love that "leads to the heights" and transfigures insofar as it is doomed in essence is not the mystical *ewig Weibliche* of the second part of Faust. It is passion in its intransigence and in its tactics with life. And it is the myth of Tristan which reappears at last!

We know quite well that *paradox* is the fundamental category of Kierkegaard's thought. Yet here is what he says in one of his most finished works, the *Philosophical Fragments:* [12]

One should not think slightingly of the paradoxical; for the paradox is the source of the thinker's passion, and the thinker without a paradox is like a lover without feeling: a paltry mediocrity. But the highest pitch of every passion is always to will its own downfall. . . . The supreme paradox of all thought is the attempt to discover something that thought cannot think.

And farther on:

Let us consider what happens in love, although it expresses the situation only imperfectly. Egoism is at the origin of the feeling for another person, but when its paradoxical passion reaches its highest pitch, the lover wishes precisely his own downfall. This is also what love wishes, hence these two powers agree in the passion of the moment, and this power is indeed love.

[12] Chapter III, "The Absolute Paradox: A Metaphysical Crotchet."

This form of thought is Tristanian.

It is first of all a form of existence, as illustrated in the doomed—but spiritually creative—relations between Kierkegaard and Regine. He can love her only at a distance, in the loss, *chosen by him*, of any presence other than a nostalgic one. (And even during the engagement he writes to apologize to her for missing an appointment: he went alone to the country that day, "to Fredensborg where memory and nostalgia coincide. It is this moment that I love so much." And he adds that when he can call her "his" in the solitude of his heart, "it is only then that we are *united*.") Regine marries someone else. The last appeal he tries to address to her—by the intermediary of her husband!—does not reach her. They meet one last time, but by accident, in the street. She greets him and he answers her greeting, but they cannot speak to each other. This is on March 7, 1855, the eve of Regine's departure for a long voyage to the Antilles. Kierkegaard dies on November 11 of the same year. Regine is across the sea, on another island.

That this form of nostalgic love and possession by loss appears both in Kierkegaard's existential dialectic and in his strictly religious thought is henceforth all too obvious for there to be any need to pursue its demonstration in terms of theology. I shall nonetheless give one example which touches the heart of my subject.

In his *Works of Love*, Kierkegaard indicates the apparently insurmountable discrepancy between love-as-passion (or poetic love), which chooses a single beloved being, and love of one's neighbor (Christian love), whose commandment is to love all men without distinction, not by an always egoistic and "carnal" elective sympathy, but in the equality of all before God. This is surprising: can this general, impersonal love that one might identify with a humanitarian social sense be truly Christian according to the Kierkegaardian conception? The development that follows re-establishes the existential requirement. The subject of "*Thou* shalt love" can be, in effect, only the Individual. Now we know that this Kierkegaardian category par excellence indicates man *isolated* by spirit—isolated from the crowd "which is deception." And the object, the neighbor—he whom one must help, according to the Gospel parable—can be, in turn, only the expression of spirit in every man. Thus only the man who has recognized and accepted himself as spirit, the man who therefore finds himself *separated* from the natural community—as though having *chosen* to lose it—can truly love his neighbor. He alone can discern, appeal to, and love in the Other the spirit which creates the Individual. This is the truly Kierkegaardian paradox. Love does not proceed from anyone to everyone, but from one man, distinguished by spirit, to each of those, whoever they are, who also exist by spirit.

But how can we help recalling here that the first mention of the Individual figures in the dedication to the *Christian Discourses* of 1843, in this form: "To the Individual whom with joy and gratitude I call *my* reader." Here was the neighbor par excellence, and—as we know from the Journals—it was Regine!

Later, the concept of Individual is (paradoxically!) universalized and enlarged. It is the signature of the spiritual man, distinguished in the anonymous crowd, sequestered by his vocation, but at the same time linked by it to the new community of spirit—and it is this man whom I call the person. Finally, this Individual is exemplified in the destiny, or more exactly in the exceptional vocation, of Sören Kierkegaard himself. A vocation which was to lead him to his doom, since he died of a long and unique passion for the inwardness of Truth.

III

NIETZSCHE AND HIS SHADOW

Two destitute lives. Two sickly bachelors, chaste though without vows, deprived of all daily affection, suffering all the torments of poetic passion, but for the Idea—adventurers of the mind only. Two existences virtually devoid of external vicissitudes. For one, the breaking-off of an engagement, the final attack against the Church, and death at forty-two. For the other, still less: a few years' professorship, a long wandering solitude, madness at forty-four. Each produced in some fifteen years his difficult, seminal work, and attracted only *in extremis*, by scandal, the attention of a few contemporaries. This external nakedness, contrasting with so much inner pathos, renders these lives exemplary: two pure tensions.

In them the action of the mythic powers perfectly reveals its slow movements of approach, of alternating emergence and eclipse.

These two chaste men meditated much on love, on woman, and on marriage. Nietzsche has certainly written less on these subjects than Kierkegaard, but his work is no less rich in brief, often brazenly contradictory judgments on these three themes. It is remarkable that Nietzsche's contradictions afford a faithful epitome of Kierkegaard's, which in their turn repeat those of Saint Paul himself!

On marriage, for example, Nietzsche suggests both the initial "difficulty" and the Husband's reply in *Stages:*

> The institution of marriage stubbornly maintains the notion that although love is a passion, it is still capable of *lasting* as a passion, and that lifelong love can be considered as the rule. By this tenacity of a noble superstition, maintained despite refutations so frequent that *they* are almost the rule, and which consequently make it a *pia fraus*, the institution has conferred upon love a superior nobility. All the institutions which have conceded passion a *belief in the latter's duration*, and the responsibility for that duration, despite the very essence of passion, have gained a new rank for it. . . .[13]

Like the Husband in *Stages*, who chose to see a supreme, even superhuman risk in the synthesis of a decision and an inclination, Nietzsche regards marriage as "a *superhuman* conception which elevates man."

But how much more precisely Kierkegaardian, by wit

[13] *The Dawn*, § 27.

as much as by tone, and by the evocation of Socrates—
is this frontal attack:

> Thus the philosopher abhors marriage and all that
> would persuade him to marriage, for he sees the married
> state as an obstacle to fulfillment. What great philosopher
> has ever been married? Heraclitus, Plato, Descartes,
> Spinoza, Leibniz, Kant, Schopenhauer—not one of them
> was married; moreover it is impossible to imagine any of
> them married. I maintain that a married philosopher
> belongs in comedy, and as for that great exception
> Socrates, it would almost seem that the malicious Soc-
> rates got married in a spirit of irony, precisely in order
> to prove that contention.[14]

"Marry, don't marry, in either case you will regret
it," Socrates said. "He who giveth in marriage doeth
well; but he that giveth not in marriage doeth better,"
Saint Paul said, speaking as a man of the Spirit—and
this is the point of view that will be personally adopted
by Kierkegaard as an Exception and by Nietzsche as
a philosopher.

Nietzsche seems more naturally misogynous than
Kierkegaard: "All the great things that have been done
by ancient humanity drew their strength from the fact
that *man* was beside *man*, and that no woman could raise
the claim to be the object of man's closest and highest
love, or even the sole object—as passion teaches." [15]
Kierkegaard, on the contrary, believes that it is by a
passionately loved woman that man raises himself,
though on condition he does not marry her.

[14] *The Genealogy of Morals*, "What Do Ascetic Ideals Mean?" § 7.
[15] *The Dawn*, § 503.

In his moments of "golden equilibrium" and creative evaluation of morality and civilization, Nietzsche puts the emphasis not on asceticism but on mastery of the instincts:

> The civilization of a people is manifested in the disciplined unity of the instincts of that people: philosophy masters the instinct of knowledge, art masters the creative instinct of forms and ecstasy, Agapè masters Eros, etc.[16]

The Agapè in question here is still, for the Greeks, merely disinterested affection, but in Nietzsche's mind it already designates that "noble" passion which since the twelfth century has glorified the values of art and enthusiasm in veneration, rather than the insistence on freedom of manners which characterizes a "slave morality."

> Now it will be understood without further explanation why love *as passion*—our European specialty— must necessarily be of noble origin. We know that its invention must be attributed to the Provençal knight-poets, those magnificent and ingenious men of *gai saber* to whom Europe owes so much, and virtually herself.[17]

Later, having listed six means of curbing the violence of the sexual instinct (avoiding opportunities, implanting discipline within the instinct, creating disgust by satiety, associating a notion of pain or shame with the instinct, dissociating and dispersing its forces, and finally physi-

---

[16] *The Birth of Philosophy in the Age of Greek Tragedy*, Chapter II.

[17] *Beyond Good and Evil*, § 260.

cally and psychically weakening and depressing oneself),
Nietzsche discovers that in reality "the *will* to combat
the violence of an instinct is beyond our power." In the
process of mastering an instinct:

> . . . the intellect is only the blind instrument of an-
> other instinct, which is the *rival* of the one whose
> violence torments us, whether it be the need for repose
> or the fear of shame and other harmful consequences,
> or love itself. Hence, while we believe we are complain-
> ing of the violence of an instinct, it is actually one
> instinct which is complaining of another.[18]

A capital passage for my argument! What Nietzsche
here calls "rival instincts" leads in fact to *two* rival
possibilities or powers in man: sexual eroticism and love.
Now neither the erotic passion of a Byron or a Napoleon
nor the love invoked here are, strictly speaking, instincts.
Eroticism begins precisely with the *noninstinctive* use of
sex (I mean the biologically nonnecessary use). And
love, which Nietzsche suggests as a possible rival instinct,
is the passion of the soul par excellence. The struggle
between the two "instincts" is therefore nothing but the
struggle between the two powers of the animistic Eros
symbolized by the myths of Don Juan and Tristan.

Let us follow the phases of their great polemic in
Nietzsche's life and work.

"By music, the passions delight in themselves." It is
curious to discover that Nietzsche, like Kierkegaard,
begins his career as an author with a work on music,

[18] *The Dawn*, § 109.

lyric tragedy, and myth: *The Birth of Tragedy*, which he publishes at the age of twenty-eight. At the same age, Kierkegaard writes *Either/Or*. And while the latter finds in Mozart's *Don Giovanni* the perfect and unique expression of passionate spontaneity, the other swears by Wagner's *Tristan* as an exemplary expression of myth and of dionysiac music.

Both regard language as incapable of translating the essence of music, in which one sees the expression of sensual spontaneity, and the other the expression of the "dionysiac spirit," or orgiastic spontaneity. For both, *"only music"* can express, in an immediate manner, the secret of Eros and its myths. But only music, too, can regenerate tragedy. "A pre-established harmony reigns between music and perfect drama."

Nietzsche sees myth in general as "the real goal of knowledge," if it is true that "the final cause of knowledge is to render existence conceivable." Myth is an "image of the world in epitome," and, without myth, "every culture is dispossessed of its natural, healthy, and creative force; only a horizon constellated with myths completes the unity of a cultural epoch. Myth alone can preserve the faculties of the imagination from the incoherence of a purposeless activity. . . . The images of myth must be invisible and omnipresent tutelary spirits favoring the development of the adolescent soul, and whose signs foretell and explain the grown man's life and struggles." [19]

[19] *The Birth of Tragedy.*

And here are the relations between the tragic myth and music:

> Tragedy absorbs the highest orgiastic music and in so doing consummates music. But then it puts beside it the tragic myth and the tragic hero. Like a mighty titan, the tragic hero shoulders the whole dionysiac world and frees us from its burdens. . . .
>
> Tragedy interposes a noble parable, *myth*, between the universality of its music and the dionysiac disposition of the spectator, and in so doing creates the illusion that music is only a supreme instrument for bringing to life the plastic world of myth. By virtue of this noble deception, it is now able to move its limbs freely in dithyrambic dance and to yield without reserve to an orgiastic abandon, an indulgence which, without this deception, it could not permit itself. Myth shields us from music while at the same time giving music its maximum freedom. In exchange, music endows the tragic myth with a convincing metaphysical significance, which the unsupported word and image could never achieve, and, moreover, assures the spectator of a supreme delight —though the way passes through annihilation and negation, so that he is made to feel that the very womb of things speaks intelligibly to him.[20]

If it were not for the words and the stage picture, Nietzsche presumes that he could not endure hearing the third act of *Tristan* "without stifling from the convulsive tension of all the fibers of his soul."

This early work marks the apogee of his friendship with Wagner and of his admiration for Schopenhauer,

[20] *Ibid.*

their common master. "I love in Wagner," he writes in 1866 to Erwin Rohde, "what I love in Schopenhauer, the ethical afflatus, the cross, death, the abyss. . . ."

But a few years later, to Peter Gast: "Long live liberty, gaiety, irresponsibility! Let us live beyond our means in order to be able to live with ourselves!"

What has happened meanwhile? On stage, at least—which means in what Nietzsche expresses consciously—Tristan has vanished and Don Juan prevails. Wagner is no longer "my noble companion in arms" but "asphyxia from the tiresome repetition of every kind of moral and religious absurdity."

Far from Basel, far from Triebschen, especially far from Bayreuth—where the creator of *Tristan* was now the happy husband of Cosima—far from the henceforth detested North, Nietzsche was living in Genoa, where he wrote *The Dawn*. "Almost every sentence of this book was conceived and virtually captured in the thousand recesses of this chaos of rocks near Genoa, where I was living alone, in a familiar intimacy with the sea." [21] He also visited Sils-Maria, in the dry air and *limpidezza* of the heights, and here he concluded the first part of *Zarathustra*, at the "holy hour"—as he later insists on specifying—of Richard Wagner's death in Venice.[22]

What does Zarathustra say? "Heedless and derisive, violent—that is how wisdom would have us. She is a

---

[21] *Ecce Homo.*

[22] The profound shock Nietzsche must have suffered at this news thus only briefly precedes the illumination at Sils-Maria, the spectacular reversal to which the second part of *Zarathustra* bears witness. Cf. *infra.*

woman. . . ." What does *The Dawn* say? "Against love
there is only one radical old remedy that is still effective:
love in return!" And what does Bizet's *Carmen* teach us,
which Nietzsche opposes "as an ironic antithesis" to the
morass, the magic, the histrionics, the Germanics, the
suspicious chastity, the decadent religiosity, and the
Sursum! Bouboum! of Wagner? *Carmen* teaches us love
"restored to its place in *nature!* Not love of an 'ideal'
woman! . . . On the contrary, love in its *fatal* aspect,
cynical, candid and cruel . . . love whose means are
war, whose basis is the *mortal hatred* of the sexes." [23]
That love which Benjamin Constant called the most
egoistic of all sentiments—"natural love" *à la* Don Juan.

There is more. Erotic Don Juanism is for Nietzsche
no more than an image, even a polemic argument, but
it is himself as philosopher, as a lover of "Wisdom,"
whom he regards as transformed into Don Juan, and
who defines himself as such!

Philosophers of the future will insist on the title of
"seducer." They will be "curious to the point of vice,
seeking with fingers that are bold to the point of cruelty,
for the ineffable . . . ready for any adventure, thanks
to an excess of free judgment. . . . Hidden beneath the
cloak of light . . . conquerors!" And their morality,
beyond good and evil, will be "the mind's dance." [24]

Here, no doubt, is the crucial text:

> A fable. —The Don Juan of knowledge: no philos-
> opher, no poet has as yet discovered him. He lacks love

[23] "The Wagner Case," in *Twilight of the Idols* (1888).
[24] *Beyond Good and Evil, passim.*

for the things he discovers, but he has wit and voluptu-
ousness, and he delights in the intrigues of knowledge
—which he pursues to the highest, remotest stars!—
until finally there is nothing left for him to hunt, save
what is absolutely painful in knowledge, like the drunk-
ard who ends up drinking absinthe and *aqua fortis*. This
is why he ends by desiring hell—it is the ultimate knowledge that *seduces* him. Perhaps it too will disappoint
him, like everything he has known! Then he will have
to stop for eternity, nailed to disappointment and himself transformed into the stone guest, and he will long
for food on the night of his knowledge, though he will
never eat again! "—For the whole world of things will
not spare a single mouthful for this starveling." [25]

The brilliant, furious rhythm, the *presto* of Don Juan,
his gay and insolent humor, the heedlessness of the *grand
seigneur* "dropping" one truth as soon as another seems
more exciting—all this dominates the collections of
aphorisms, from *Human, All Too Human* to *The Gay
Science* and *The Genealogy of Morals*.

But as early as *The Dawn*, this Don Juan of knowledge questions himself, which is not one of his typical
characteristics. Or perhaps he wants to go farther in this
direction, swept on by his frenzy of discoveries and
triumphant negations? The last one will cast him into
the very thing whose rejection he incarnated:

The New Passion. —Why do we fear and hate the
possibility of a return to barbarism? Because barbarism
would make men more unhappy than they are? Alas no!
The barbarians were always happier: let us make no
mistake about that. —But it is our *instinct of knowledge*

[25] *The Dawn*, § 327.

that is too highly developed for us to be able to appreciate happiness without knowledge, or happiness that comes from a solid and vigorous illusion; we suffer from even imagining such a state of affairs! The restlessness of discovery and divination has assumed as much charm for us, has become as indispensable as unhappy love for the lover: nothing in the world would persuade him to abandon it for a state of indifference;—yes, perhaps we, too, are doomed lovers. In us, knowledge has been transformed into passion which fears no sacrifice; which has, indeed, only one fear, that of dying out. . . .

But suppose the passion for knowledge extinguishes humanity? Let it! "Even this thought has no power over us. Was Christianity ever afraid of such ideas? Are not *passion and death* twin sisters?" [26]

In an ecstasy of defiance, Don Juan has discovered his old adversary's secret truth. Who knows if he is not about to *love it?*

In the third part of *Thus Spake Zarathustra* occurs the transformation scene prepared by these various dissonant chords, whose muffled interrogation could not fail to awaken in Nietzsche's memory the Tristanian motifs of Desire, Invocation to the Night, and Deliverance from Time and Ecstasy.

Suddenly it is the Shadow, his shadow, that speaks:

> *O man, take care!*
> *What does the deep midnight declare?*
> *"I was asleep—*
> *From a deep dream I woke and swear:*

[26] *Ibid.*, § 429.

The world is deep,
Deeper than day had been aware.
Deep is its woe;
But joy deeper still than agony;
Woe implores: Go!
But all joy wants eternity—
Wants deep, wants deep eternity!"

This is the "New Passion" heralded by the fragment of *The Dawn:* it is the return of the mortal myth of love which transfixes and transfigures. It is the Midnight Song greeting Eternity, when Don Juan dies with time and the succession of moments. It is the vision of the Eternal Return that suddenly "nails" the Don Juan of knowledge. It is Nietzsche himself who holds out his hand to the Commendatore—to the Eternal Ghost, to the Father! —in a supreme challenge, and in order to go down to his ruin.

And this will shortly be the almost posthumous confession, the last appeal to Isolde, the note that he writes to Cosima the day his madness is upon him: "Ariadne, I love you! signed: Dionysos."

"The Wagner Case"—which is a last anti-Tristan act —had just been sent to the printer.

In *The Dawn*, I read again: "Let the man who wishes to kill his enemy consider whether this is not a way of perpetuating that enemy in himself."

The "Nietzsche Case" has not been solved by madness. And no one has formulated its *données* better than Nietzsche himself.

The last aphorism of *The Dawn* ends as follows:

> Where do we want to go? Do we want to cross the
> sea? Where does this powerful passion lead, that takes
> precedence over every other? Why this frenzied flight
> always in this same direction, toward the point where
> until now every sun *waned* and *went out?* Perhaps some
> day it will be said that we too, steering always for the
> west, hoped to reach an unknown Indies—but that it
> was our destiny to founder before the infinite? Or else,
> my brothers—or else?

In *Ecce Homo*, Nietzsche comments: "This book
ends with an 'Or else?'—it is the only book in the world
that ends with 'Or else?' "

He was no doubt unaware that thirty-eight years
earlier, a book had appeared in Denmark with the title
Either/Or (*Enten-Eller*), a book that can be epitomized
by this alternative:—either Don Juan, or else the Tristan
of Faith.

Was it really Nietzsche's *destiny* "to founder before
the infinite"? Or on the contrary his deliberate choice?
Or else . . . has he reached the "unknown Indies"?

IV

ALTERNATIVE OR ALTERNATION?

The Don Juan-Tristan antinomy, as I have formulated
it elsewhere, may here be summarized in a few sentences:

> Let us consider the Don Juan of the theater as Tris-
> tan's inverse reflection.

The contrast consists first of all in the external aspect of the characters, in their rhythm. We imagine Don Juan always booted and spurred, ready to leap forward if he happens to stop for a moment in his course. On the contrary, Tristan comes on stage with the somnambulistic slowness of a man hypnotized by a marvelous, inexhaustibly fascinating object. One possessed a thousand and three women (in Spain alone), the other only one. But it is multiplicity that is impoverished, while the entire world is concentrated in a single being infinitely possessed. Tristan no longer needs the world—because he loves! While Don Juan, always loved, cannot love in return. Hence his anguish and his frenzied course.

The one seeks in the act of love the pleasure of a profanation, the other accomplishes the sanctifying "exploit" by remaining chaste. Don Juan's tactic is rape, and as soon as his victory is won, he abandons the field. Now the rules of courtly love made rape the crime of crimes, the unforgivable felony, and declared homage a commitment to the death. Don Juan thus makes himself a tributary of the very morality he abuses. It must exist so he may violate it. Tristan is liberated from the interaction of rules, sins, and virtues by the grace of a virtue that transcends the world of law.

Ultimately everything comes down to this opposition: Don Juan is the demon of pure immanence, the prisoner of the world's appearances, the martyr of increasingly disappointing and contemptible sensation—while Tristan is the prisoner of timelessness—*beyond day and night*— the martyr of a rapture which is transformed into pure joy upon death.

We may note further: Don Juan jokes, laughs aloud, provokes death when the Commendatore holds out his hand to him in Mozart's last act, by an ultimate defiance compensating for acts of baseness that would have dishonored a true knight. Tristan, melancholy and brave, abdicates his pride, on the contrary, only at the approach of luminous death.

I find they share only one characteristic: both have swords in their hand.[27]

Or simply in a few words: Tristan, woeful time, joyous eternity. —Don Juan, joyous moments, an eternity of hell.

So pure a contrast, term against term, obviously implies an interacting link; much more: a complementary relation in the sense of present-day physics. Don Juan is inconceivable without Tristan, and without him would not have appeared in the world. But this link of reciprocal genesis cannot be expressed in the same way in terms of history, ethics, or psychology.

History indicates the *filiation* of the myths, then their reappearances, and lastly their *statistical coexistence* in the whole of a society as complex as ours.

Ethics condemns both myths in principle. In fact, it demands that if one asserts its virtue, it be at the price of the radical exclusion of the other. (Worse than a Don Juan, worse than a Tristan, would be a married Don Juan or a promiscuous Tristan.)

Psychology perceives that every *appearance* of one of the myths on the level of individual consciousness corresponds to the *occultation* of the other in the unconscious. The possibility of an inversion of the relation therefore remains a permanent one. Further, insofar as behavior, thought, and emotion are dissociated in the

---

[27] *Love in the Western World*, rev. ed., Book IV, Chapter 13.

same individual, Don Juan can dominate any one of the three, Tristan any other.

The filiation of the myths raises no problems. The legend of Tristan dates from the twelfth century, that of Don Juan goes back only as far as the Renaissance, and was actually constituted only by means of the temporary repression of the "noble" passion Nietzsche spoke of, during the Age of Enlightenment. "As we see, by closing our eyes, a black statue in place of the white one we have just considered, the eclipse of the myth of passion was to bring Tristan's antithesis to light. If Don Juan is not, historically, an invention of the eighteenth century, at least this period has played with regard to this character the same role as Lucifer with regard to the Creation in Manichean doctrine: it has given Molina's *Burlador* its own likeness and stamped him forever with two features entirely characteristic of itself: *wickedness* and *rascality*. A perfect antithesis of the two virtues of knightly love: candor and courtesy." [28]

Let us also note that Don Juan normally follows Tristan, as the cosmopolitan succeeds the feudal. If Tristan leaves his estates, withdraws from the court, his "errantry" translates the Quest, the Spiritual Exile into terms of Space. But Don Juan's migrant humor is merely nomadism; it expresses the enlightened rationalist's systematic infidelity to the customs, prejudices, and principles of the native group, the tribe, or the nation. This is why the reappearance of "mortal passion" toward the middle of the nineteenth century, if it is initially the

[28] *Ibid.*

144

result of romanticism, coincides quite deliberately with the first impulse of nationalist passion, which is its transposition on the political level.[29]

But Don Juan's nomadism is not only cosmopolitan and therefore modern. The hero's successes, like Casanova's, are not only the result of individual charm. Ancestral customs, forgotten for centuries, are suddenly reactivated by his attributes as a stranger. To the question of a woman whom he is trying to seduce: "Ah, Heaven! Man, who art thou?" Tirso de Molina's Don Juan answers: "Who am I? A man without a name." This *man without a name*, without a past, without a future, is one of the riders from the times when the nomad hordes suddenly appeared on the lands of the first settlers, pillaged, raped their women, taught them pleasure in the keenness of dread, and galloped back to their wasteland. And he is also the priest or the divine

[29] The opportunist politician derives from the Don Juanesque type. At the other extreme, General De Gaulle is Tristanian in his nationalism. His Iseult is France, as he comes close to saying in more than one page of his *Memoirs,* and not only in the first sentences where he compares France to the "fairy-tale princess . . . dedicated to an eminent and exceptional fate," even to "exemplary misfortunes." For years he loved her from afar, in his exile. He restored her to her legitimate Husband, represented by the Legality of the State, after having delivered her in battle from the giant who held her captive and who demanded his tribute of young men (Minotaur-Morholt-Hitler). Then he was obliged to withdraw again, disgusted by the plotting of the felonious barons. Naturally he returned at her call. But the true Tristanian passion is nourished on withdrawals and obstacles, even provoking them if they appear to be lacking. Between France and himself, when he was the strongest—Tristan stronger than King Mark—did he not lay a symbolic *sword?* In order for a passion of this nature not to conclude in some "exemplary misfortune," there must be some happy "accident of history" to counteract the logic of the Myth.

hero in the ancient primitive religions: the man who is holy or strong enough to dare to assume the supposed dangers of the act of defloration—perils of the soul, loss of *mana*. Thus the *jus primae noctis* was really a kind of "religious" duty for the *seigneur*. At night, masked, outlaw or angel, "the man without a name" comes *from elsewhere*, passes through, embraces, says *the word*, reveals, and vanishes. Don Ottavio rages in the name of morality, but the peasant Masetto seems to know something of what is going on. In this one sense, Don Juan proceeds from a state of civilization far anterior to Christianity and still farther from courtly chivalry.

From the point of view of individual psychology, Tristan's precedence appears still more obvious. Love-as-passion is experienced in all its animistic purity only by early adolescence. It is absolute emotion, pure pain-joy, and will never be as clearly distinct from any other pain or joy. The sentiment which the troubadours express is typically adolescent, and almost independent of sex. If it manages to fix upon a single being without insurmountable obstacles, it normally leads to marriage, that is, to the point of departure of one of the most complex dialectics, whose basic terms are the sexual, the emotional, and the social. Let us suppose that the synthesis of the three terms occurs, and that what results is a *true couple*. This means that at the heart of this new entity, the relations among the three terms—sexual exchanges, affective exchanges, exchanges with society—have found their regimen of equilibrium in movement and that the result of this system of exchanges is positive for both of the persons composing the couple. Such a synthesis can become more or less stable, but cannot be static in any case, in the sense in which social morality and its secular or religious laws accept it. For it will soon be put to the *unforeseen* test of duration, which necessarily modifies the relative importance of each of the three terms, and this in two different beings. (Calculate the number of possible permutations and combinations: this is not my subject, but that of a treatise on marriage.)

If, on the contrary, emotion, in its impulse toward marriage, is blocked by insurmountable objects, which are generally of a social nature, it either exalts itself and denies them—or renounces and hates them. Soon magnetized by sex, emotion assumes a new energy, or new reasons to renounce itself. It is at this point that the myths seize upon it. In both cases, marriage is condemned: since it is social duration, one of the two myths tends to transcend, the other to prey upon it. One demands more, infinitely more, in the direction of emotion-as-passion: it therefore opposes duration with an angelic eternity. The other claims that sex is enough: to duration it opposes only the moment of the erotic encounter. From this point of view, Tristan is a husband *manqué* because he lacks social feeling and overcompensates this lack by passion; while Don Juan is a Tristan *manqué*, because he has retreated from both the social and the emotional.[30]

---

[30] Nietzsche observes: "The man who cannot find the road which leads to *his* ideal lives more frivolously, more insolently than the man without an ideal." (*Beyond Good and Evil*, § 133.)

But since there is virtually no marriage which succeeds in maintaining a *synthesis in duration* of the various elements whose excess or failure is symbolized by our two myths, most real couples are subject in their crises to the action of one of the two.

Morality and society then deliver their imperatives. If these suffice to maintain the couple's equilibrium, myth-analysis has nothing further to say. If they lead to divorce or shock treatment, it asks to be heard: not as a psychiatrist or as a priest, not as a lawyer and still less as a judge, but simply because it recognizes the *invisible protagonists* of the always latent drama who have just revealed themselves.

First, then, we have had to specify the *contrast* of the two most compelling myths to which the Western psyche is subject. The civilizing, organizing, and dynamic function which they can also have requires an objective awareness of their true nature, and of the goals toward which their structures lead us.

From the point of view of history and psychology—phylogenesis, ontogenesis—it is the *alternation* of the myths which is manifest—their genetic interdependence and their dialectical coexistence—one acting in the shadows when the other functions in daylight. Any diagnosis of a situation, any prognosis as to its development, must therefore be established on this basis. The same is true for a personal life considered in its biographical duration: the examples given here have established the fact.

On the other hand, in the hours of crisis which bachelors too sometimes suffer, it is in the form of an *alternative* that the drama imposes itself, that it is experienced, and that morality formulates its demands. Now one cannot deal with an alternative except by knowing the goals which each of its terms prescribes and to which it inclines us, according to its law.

But perhaps these goals, once they are recognized, turn out to be essentially complementary. Then it would no longer be a matter of resolving a dilemma, but of restoring a tension in all its vital equilibrium.

V

ULTIMATE MEANING OF THE TWO MYTHS

What are the goals of our lives beyond survival, work, and making money, which are actually only means? Let us limit ourselves to these four: duration, happiness, freedom, love.

DURATION. Any man who obtains what he desires, or who is about to obtain it, seeks duration: nothing is more natural than the vows and promises lavished by lovers. Spontaneous happiness seeks duration. But duration engenders boredom: this is why many confuse the two. I conceive, nonetheless, two nonmediocre reasons for refusing normal duration; or rather two temperaments that can never accommodate themselves to it. One

requires a constantly increased intensity, the other an
ever-new excitation. One will seek drama, the other
surprise. Whether this is a reaction to an incapacity to
relate love and normal existence, or a preference for
excess in itself, the one will claim to transcend, the other
to despise duration. One will tend to be Tristan, the
other Don Juan.

Don Juan sings that he is happy only in the moment,
in novelty, and in change, and that he has never asked
for more. "To believe him unhappy because he goes
from one to another is to believe him unhappy because
he does not achieve a goal he does not pursue," writes
one of his apologists,[31] who immediately adds: "He is
happy even in the failures of his pursuit, because his
pleasure is in pursuit rather than in capture." The *excitation* of pursuit is enough for him, is even, we are told,
the "essential" for him. This "natural instinct of the
male" is also a "rational instinct." (Let us note this in-
novation in passing.) "I have picked an apple; I have
enjoyed it. I see another: nothing more rational than
to pick it too." It is true that Don Juan "reasons" like
this in each of us, at times. This is because he forgets
that a woman is not an apple. And that she will be
mortally offended by the man who has not "captured"
her, who has been content to "taste" her. Donna Anna
pursues Don Juan with her hatred because, according to
the primitive legend—as Otto Rank reminds us—"he has
not given her the soul he owes her . . . he has deceived
the woman in her, abusing his divine role as animator

[31] Henri de Montherlant, *Sur les Femmes.*

merely in order to satisfy the pleasure of his senses." [32]
All sexual magic aside, when the "divine" is reduced to
the human and the soul no longer identified with the
spirit or the person, the meaning is clear: Don Juan's
rejection of duration is equivalent to the rejection of
true possession, which implies exchange and giving, at
least between human beings; such things are not over
and done with so quickly!

It is only fair to point out, moreover, that the apple-
eating Don Juan just cited remains a little short of the
mark. He will never accede to eroticism, which is the
transcendence of instinct and of animal hungers. His
affairs are no more interesting than other people's cou-
plings, and have no glamour for the imagination. Mozart
could have done nothing with him, nor even Da Ponte.
He serves here as an extreme example, to reveal a certain
inner weakness of Don Juanesque eroticism, even in its
loftiest and most fascinating manifestations for the mind.
He also reminds us that duration is not only the reality
of the couple, but that of the desired *object*. Most erotic
reverie founders on the discovery that the human object
is still alive, still endures, and remains the same (with all
that may be embarrassing or intolerable about such per-

[32] *Die Don-Juan Gestalt*, 1922. Apropos of Donna Anna: Mozart's
biographers assure us that his contemporaries did not doubt for a
moment that Donna Anna had yielded to Don Juan, taking (or not)
"the unknown man" for her fiancé, under cover of darkness. But it
is Donna Anna who calls her father, at the moment she senses Don
Juan is about to run away, a little too quickly. I do not see Casanova
"betrayed" in this way. He enjoyed his conquests better and they
"conquered" him better: in his *Mémoires*, separations leave each
party happy. We may also note that Donna Anna, if she declares her
hatred for Don Juan, is in no hurry to marry Don Ottavio.

sistence) *after* the fulfillment of the exciting fantasy. And this is why the Empress Theodora had her one-night lovers killed before dawn.

Tristan, on the contrary, wants eternity, for he wants to escape suffering, and suffering is linked to time and space, which modify, distinguish, and separate—*"but all joy wants eternity, wants deep, wants deep eternity."* Such is the form of his escape, of his refusal of incarnated duration. He wants *more*, and not *less*, than marriage; more, and not less, than the possession of "the truth in a soul and a body," as Rimbaud puts it. He finds the excitation of novelty in the renewed drama of a single passion that is ever more intense, burning up life itself. Psychosis or spirituality? Weakness, or true strength? Only a sure estimate of our life in this world, and of its meaning or its absurdity, will put us in a position to answer.

If our present incarnation is only suffering and illusion —suffering on account of illusion, according to Buddhism—it is Tristan who is right, and marriage wrong.

If there is no other life, if reality is historical, material, and biological, marriage is a civic duty, and Don Juan would then be freedom, an inverted reflection of the spirit he denies.

One might also believe that marriage is "the fulfillment of time" as the Husband in Kierkegaard says, the living synthesis of the moment, duration, and eternity. Only the man who has solved this problem in his life is in a position to condemn Don Juan and Tristan both; but he no longer has any reason to do so.

HAPPINESS.   Moments of great pleasure multiplied by endless adventures, couples happy in the duration of their love, ecstatic torments of passion: the argument of happiness serves for all. Nor is this a reason for it to be false. Still, it cannot prevent the sneers of those whom boredom, satiety, jealousy, betrayal, frustration or impotence, solitude or the obsession of desertion, anguish or vulgarity of mind and soul—these two cases are the most common—prevent from playing a "happy" role in marriage, in libertinage, or in passion. Not to mention the resentment each of the three types, even when successful, feels toward the other two: "I was born for this or that (the contrary of what I am actually experiencing), I have always dreamed of . . . if I could live my life over again. . . ."

But to dream of something else is normal. A certain duality is normal, insofar as it merely translates the formula of *life* on all levels: spiritual, animistic, biological, and physical. As a matter of fact, no life is conceivable apart from permanent tension, even the battle (whether latent or overt) between at least *two* antagonistic tendencies.

Let us take an elementary and primordial example, that of the life of a cell. We know today that this life depends on the simultaneous action of *two* nucleic acids, concentrated in the nucleus but also at work in the cytoplasm, where they are the induction agents of the synthesis of proteins. As long as both are active, the cell functions well, its system of exchanges and syntheses is creative: one might say that it is "happy." But suppose a virus penetrates the cell: the cell digests, disintegrates, and assimilates it—it is no longer there, materially. And then some minutes or hours later, it is the cell itself, modified in its "soul" (that is, in the program of activity of which its chromosomes are the carriers), which begins to fabricate the vanished virus—until it dies by explosion, infecting the neighboring cells. This is how contagion is propagated within an organ. But after all, what is a virus? That is the point. A virus is a composite of substances analogous to those of the cell, except that it contains *only one* of the nucleic acids. This accounts for all its harmfulness. (Let us also remark that the virus cannot propagate itself and reproduce save at the expense of living cells: without them, it cannot subsist.)

Let us now imagine an individual soul or even a couple, that "social cell": [33] its happiness will be conditioned by the presence of two antagonistic tendencies, and its duration will be the product of the syntheses which they permanently induce. If one of the myths manages to convince and modify the secret heart, the "nucleus" of this soul, then we have the symptoms of neurosis, the drama and explosion of the couple. If, on the contrary, the soul resists, it will henceforth be immunized. Or else the noxious effect of the myth is merely kept latent, capable of reviving under the effect of an emotive shock.

This biological analogy does not, of course, explain the nature *in itself* of our myths, which are phenomena of the soul. But it helps us to conceive the process of

[33] Paul Bourget.

their action more clearly; perhaps, too, of their apparent eclipses and sudden recurrences during the course of a life. (I am thinking, for instance, of the shock Nietzsche suffered on hearing of Wagner's death: the Tristan motif reappears soon after in the second part of *Zarathustra:* "For I love thee, O eternity!")

A certain formal dialectic being common to all the phenomena which derive from life in general, why reject the hypothesis that the "morbid" agents also behave in a manner formally analogous, whatever the level of life considered? I shall cite—and in passing—only one example of this same dialectic applied to political life.

Totalitarianism is characterized by its all-inclusive claims and by its refusal to compromise with any kind of opposition. What distinguishes it from any other system—whatever its resemblances to several of them— is, precisely, that it admits only *one* tendency, universal centralization. Federalism, on the contrary, is defined as the perpetual synthesis of *two* antagonistic tendencies: the central authority and regional autonomy, union and diversity. Federalism represents the health of the body politic, or its happiness; totalitarianism, its mortal illness. Having lived nearly a year in Hitler's Germany, I was accustomed to answer those who questioned me as to the motives for the *real* adherence of so many Germans to an obviously lunatic doctrine: "I have seen certain students of mine become Nazis. I have seen them change physically. They assumed those severe expressions, that 'objective' stare, that pale coloring, that heaviness in the lower part of the face which allows us to recognize a

Nazi leader at first glance. However frivolous this may seem to you, I believe that totalitarianism is a *virus*, and if you catch it, there is nothing you can do." I didn't know how right I was.[34]

FREEDOM. With the first measures of the offstage minuet—the music comes from inside the palace—the three avenging Masks advance and Don Giovanni invites them in, provoking fate. (There can be no doubt that he has recognized them.) The tragic party begins, the excitement increases, the orchestra multiplies its appeals to pleasure. (We are now in the palace.) Suddenly everything stops upon the trio's entrance. A few powerful chords, an exchange of greetings as one might cross swords, every sense alert, and Don Giovanni exclaims loudly:

> È aperto a tutti quanti,
> Viva la libertà!

> (Everyone is welcome!
> Hurrah for freedom!)

And then the startling thing: *all the voices* return this challenge, each taking it up in his own key! The three Masks, Zerlina, and her fiancé join Don Giovanni and Leporello. *Viva la libertà* bursts forth twelve times over, shouted out by different voices, in alternation or to-

---

[34] My *Journal d'Allemagne* makes only one or two covert allusions to this physical transformation. Apparently my hypothesis could be read between the lines nonetheless, since Eugène Ionesco has said that my book suggested the subject of his *Rhinoceros* to him.

gether, until the final *tutti* in a triumphant harmony! But what can this harmony signify? For the Masks, freedom means killing the seducer and making themselves the instruments of a fate which terrifies them; for the valet, it means serving his master as long as he is paid, and betraying him if things go badly; for Masetto, it means keeping Zerlina from yielding to the *seigneur's* enterprises; for Zerlina, it means yielding; and for Don Giovanni it means conquering. Here, then, the morality of principles, the morality of slaves, and the morality of masters together demand and insist on their freedom, and each of these freedoms contradicts the other, and all, in various degrees, merely serve the order assigned to each. Finally, they are all singing: Hurrah for the law! The only exception is the freedom of Don Giovanni, who leads the chorus: his freedom will defy fate, but succumb to it. Yet only this freedom interests us; the others are merely claims determined by social standing or utilitarian ethics. Then is there no freedom? Or is the only true freedom in the libertine's defiance of all that ordinary men hold as true, necessary, and sacred?

"When the Christian crusaders in the East happened upon the invincible Society of Assassins," Nietzsche wrote in a Don Juanesque mood, "they must have got some hint of the slogan reserved for the highest ranks, which ran, *Nothing is true; everything is permitted.* Here we have real freedom, for the notion of truth itself has been disposed of." [35]

[35] *The Genealogy of Morals,* Part III, § 24.

157

One cannot go further, one cannot go higher—but perhaps this is going too high—in the defense and illustration of intellectual libertinage, on the one hand against Christian freedom, which is *obedience* to what has been revealed, and on the other against scientific asceticism, which is also, in its way, a *faith* in the truly objective, an obedience to the verifiable. Yet the freedom Nietzsche wants to love will quickly cease being desirable when he has killed truth itself: no "true" freedom without truth.

As Nietzsche shows—though only to forget it once he attacks the Christian, metaphysical, and ascetic spirit and scientific "*petit-faitalisme*"—the formula "Nothing is true; everything is permitted" is a knowledge apart, a religious datum and a mystical symbol. "All is permitted," Saint Paul declares. "Love and do what thou wilt," Augustine says. The Hindu and Buddhist East has not said anything different before them, nor the mystics of Islam since. Such knowledge cannot be achieved by a defiance of everyday morality, or even by a revolt against the law, to which all true spiritual men are "dead . . . wherein we should serve in newness of spirit, and not in the oldness of the letter." [36] This, the only "true" freedom, cannot be the term for any kind of assertion, which is necessarily made upon (against) the outer world, the constituted truths: for these are not "true" (if they are frequently useful) and their overthrow would not be enough to reveal the truth, still less to refute it.

[36] Romans 7:6.

Achieving true freedom implies an inner change—instantaneous, as in Christian conversion and Buddhist illumination, or slowly acquired, as in Yoga. Achieving true freedom must imply a *liberation*.

Liberation is Tristan's way. His passion seeks to love without limits, outside of forms and time, above the separate and desiring self, beyond all earthly attachments—it seeks that heaven where lover and beloved are identified in a single being, in the endless kingdom of love that knows no awakening. There nothing is true or false, nor thine or mine, nor separate or forbidden, in the nameless One:

> *In dem wogenden Schwall*
> *in dem tönenden Schall*
> *in des Welt Atems wehendem All*
> > *ertrinken*
> > *versinken*
> > *unbewusst*
> > *höchste Lust!* [37]

(In the swelling flood
in the echoing sound
in the infinite torment of the World's breath,
> be engulfed
> sink deep
> unknowing
> supreme joy!)

But if the self is transcended, *who* is free? And *who* can still love *whom?* It is in the never-resolved enigma of this romantic Nirvana (where the World's breath is

[37] Last lines of the libretto of *Tristan und Isolde*.

still a "torment"!) that the last measures of *Tristan* leave us.

LOVE. Here the dialectic of the two myths is condensed. It achieves its most abstract formulation when it finally overtakes what was supposed to be its concrete origin, and which escapes it.

No love for Don Juan, only desire; and not for his "neighbor" but only for objects. But for Tristan, if the last obstacle that nourishes his passion is the separate self, and if this self must sink into the all-encompassing unconscious, there is neither object nor "neighbor." There is nothing but the love of love in a subject which must also vanish. What is left? As others lose, to save their life, the reasons for living, Tristan loses, on account of love, the human reasons for loving.

In the purity of their mythic expression, Don Juan's extraversion and Tristan's introversion annihilate the reality of the "neighbor," each in its own way. Symbols of the soul, Don Juan and Tristan are in fact only two ways of loving without loving one's neighbor. Not being persons, but powers, they cannot love themselves, which is the condition of loving anyone else, and therefore of any real love: for without a "neighbor," love no longer knows where to begin.

All true love is a *reciprocal relation*. This relation is first established within each person, between the individual, who is the natural object, and the vocation which he receives, a new subject—and such is love of oneself. It is next established within the couple, between the two subject-objects which the married persons constitute. Lastly, it is established between the couple and the human community.

Such is the fulfillment of love—and its marvelous rarity! But our arts have always retreated before it. And our literatures, impotent to create the myth of ideal marriage, have lived on its diseases.

At this point of a long meditation at the fabulous crossroads not indicated on any map, a conclusion—and one that does not entirely surprise us—at last unmasks its ambiguous countenance.

The two most compelling myths of love the West has created are in reality two negations of true love in marriage, though they are inseparable from it: they are born of it, against it, and cannot perpetuate themselves without it.

But here they reveal at the same time their function which is or has become so vital in our development. They are not only our major temptations, but *signs* charged with meaning. Once they suddenly appear before us, fascinating as a dream of other nights, instead of accompanying us into the shadow, we know that the moment has come to round the cape, or else to confront the tempest and the longed-for storms.

Both triumph over life, as soon as it relaxes its tensions. Both triumph over love, as soon as it withdraws into itself, ceasing to be a living exchange. Lastly, both triumph over our mass-produced, antiseptic, socialized moralities that have neither style nor *virtù*. Once an imbalance betrays itself in us, or provokes a crisis in the couple, they hurl themselves upon it and aggravate it wantonly. Let one of them gain the upper hand and it will make short work of marriage, moderation, the human person, and life itself. Yet without them, what would our loves be?

DIALECTIC OF THE MYTHS (II)

The Two Souls of André Gide

"now that I see a little more clearly . . ."
Et Nunc Manet In Te

AFTER André Gide's death, I contributed to a collective *Hommage* several pages whose personal tone seemed appropriate to the occasion. I reprint them here without alteration, not because they deserve this in themselves, quite the contrary; it is their inadequacy that interests me, a certain blurred outlook, certain errors of perspective and their possible correction by a better-informed consideration. Here is the problem: can a more intimate knowledge of the myths permit a more accurate acquaintance with someone who has lived before your eyes, who has spoken of himself a great deal and made confessions to you which you supposed you understood, but who perhaps was as much deceived about himself as you were? An affirmative answer to this question would go far to confirm, by collation, my essays in mythanalysis dealing with persons whom I have not known and with fictional characters who are thereby unable to refute me.

A PROTESTANT CONSPIRACY

Actually, we knew each other only slightly on that day in June 1939, when I saw him coming downstairs into the lobby of the Gallimard offices where I was making a telephone call. I went on talking, watching him out of the corner of my eye. He stopped, seemed to be waiting. I put down the receiver, and we walked out together. We sat on a bench of the Boulevard Saint-Germain. The cars passed close by. Over the din, he articulated: "Where are you living now?" I yelled that I had to leave Charles du Bos's house the next day since he was returning from America, and that I had just heard that the possibility of another apartment had fallen through. Then he said again (but it was hard to be sure of what I heard): "You're looking for a studio?" "Yes, that's just what I need." He looked surprised, then amused. And suddenly, as he stood up: "Well, let's go have a look at it right now!" Only then did I realize he had said: "I have a studio. . . ."

The next day, we arrived at his house very early in the morning. The studio was enormous and attractive, with a staircase leading to a good-sized upper gallery. Through a quilted door from the library where he worked, Gide appeared in a gray dressing gown, his body rather thickset, his shoulders broad, his splendid Tibetan monk's head barred with a thin yet friendly smile. It was a very warm day. He took two bottles of beer out of his pockets and offered them to us. A trapeze was hanging in the middle of the studio. Gide leaned both hands on it and balanced there, looking at our suitcases. "It's all been arranged so suddenly," he said. "It's peculiar . . . almost enough to make me believe in Providence! . . . But once people find out you're living here, what will they say? . . ." And through clenched teeth he repeated: "What will people say? . . ." with an inquisitorial smile. I was careful not to answer. Finally Gide, laughing: "They'll say it's a Protestant conspiracy!"

The remark had a certain pertinence. Every morning, around eleven, he opened the quilted door, announcing himself by a deep "*Allô! Allô!*" and asked me to come into the library for a few moments. Each time he brought the conversation around to religious or even theological subjects, as if it was just to talk about them that he had offered me his hospitality.

Saint Paul was still his *bête noire*. And the very notion of orthodoxy. He vigorously denied that the expression "Protestant orthodoxy" could have any meaning. For him, the Protestant was the dissenter (as is generally believed in France). The fruitful constraints he once insisted on in art, the "dogmatic criticism" of the great ages, were no more than lies for him in questions of a religious order. Perhaps he was concerned with morality alone? "On the whole," I said, "you're content with the liberal Protestantism of the late nineteenth century?" "Yes, more or less, the position of Pastor Roberty, whom I was very fond of."

Quickly bored by intellectual discussion, he seemed to reject all thought that hadn't first attracted him by its style. He often spoke of Bossuet's *Variations* with lively admiration, but objected to Kierkegaard, whom he called "too long-winded." Thus candidly declaring his limits, and the particular means of his explorations.

I took notes on only one of these conversations, that of June 20. I had had the impression, that day, that Gide laid aside discretion in his avowals, that he told me what he couldn't say, and has perhaps never repeated.

The conversation began about *Love in the Western*

World, which he was reading [1] and in which, to my profound surprise, he said he had found an explanation for the "errors of his youth." In slow and over-particular sentences, broken by sniffs and silences, he began talking about the "drama of his life."

As a young man, in love and puritanical, he had tried to dissociate love and pleasure. He believed that "heterosexual love" was all the purer if it had nothing carnal about it.[2] "That's how I completely misled myself!" he repeated, accenting the verb. What often struck him about women was the way they "took offense at a man's desire for them." Several married women confided to him "that they regarded their husbands' libido as something morbid. 'It keeps starting over again all the time!' they said." He shook his head—"It's all very odd, don't you think?"—a glint of malice in the corner of his eye. Then he made several obscure remarks that apparently contradicted what he had just said: "It took me too long to get over the illusion that woman has no need of physical intercourse, not as much as we. . . . Unfortunately, I didn't see clearly. . . . That's how you deceive yourself, and the consequences. . . . I was *stupid* enough to believe such a thing! Never believe what women tell you. . . ." Then his expression grew tense and anxious. "I'm talking to you quite sincerely, I'm telling you about

[1] "You're going to believe I'm obsessed," he said, laughing, "but I can't help thinking that your troubadours were mostly homosexuals." I answered that several of them were, as a matter of fact.

[2] In 1960, I read in *Et Nunc Manet In Te:* "I had no difficulty proving elsewhere that I wasn't incapable of ardor (I mean the ardor that procreates), but on condition that nothing intellectual or sentimental was involved."

things that have played a very serious role in my life."
(I was struck by the confessional tone, by the "that-was-bad" tenor of his remarks.) And suddenly, after a pause:
"It's what shunted me, at that period—I mean my first trip to Africa—onto a terribly wrong track."

Then he coughed, complained that he smoked too much and could never restrain himself.

The following days, he gave me to read, in signatures, the proofs of his *Journal* on which I was to write an article for the *Nouvelle Revue Française*. He insisted—as only he knew how!—on the suppressions he had made. All the passages that intimately concerned his wife—"the only being," he said, "whom I truly loved"—had been cut. They were to be read later. He had copied them out in two gray schoolboy notebooks.

One evening he came to tell me he planned to be away for eight days. But his library would be at my disposal; I should come and take any books I might need.

The next day, I went in, of course. There were dust covers over the furniture, a kind of old sheet covering his huge desk. On top of it, very much in evidence, a thick gray schoolboy notebook. I read the first lines, to make sure, and quickly closed the cover. Discretion, or fear of falling into the trap? Both, probably.

How many times did I see him again after the war? Often, actually, and in various places: in his Paris apartment; near Lausanne; in Neuchâtel; in Berne. But I have no recollection of any conversation that deserves recounting—none that in any way modifies his familiar image. We talked about style, phrasing, Littré. And some-times about literature. (But he was obviously turning away from literature, no longer caring much for any-thing except works he felt least capable of writing: those of a Marcel Aymé, a Simenon.) In Berne, during a lunch, he rather insistently asked my opinion of Strindberg, and I gave him a rather vague answer, surprised by the ques-tion more than anything else. Eight days later, he re-ceived the Nobel Prize.

One evening in Neuchâtel, at a mutual friend's, we played the *cadavre exquis* parlor game. One player writes down three questions while at the same time the other writes three answers, then the papers are read aloud. A game of telepathy rather than a *jeu de hasard*. My last question was: "What is style?" His daughter Catherine read her last answer: "The Biped's originality." ("The Biped" was his nickname in the group.) Gide remarked loudly that the game was becoming too personal, and suggested doggerel verses. "Since I'm especially good at them!" he announced.

Few men have given me the impression that the reli-gious problem existed in their lives as a permanent *prob-lem*. Sidetracked, suppressed in some; and in others solved, they suppose. I'm not saying it tortured Gide, aside from several crises for which we have his testi-mony, but it remained, for him, a problem.

Gide had little religious instinct, and still less taste for metaphysics. He preferred what he considered important to what others considered profound. His lack of poetic sense seems to me almost unmatched since Montaigne. (I don't deny his lyricism for a moment.) And this was how he managed to replace the tragic sense by perplexity. All of which may illuminate his attitude toward Christianity and its mystery.

Can we deny religious instinct to this man, when Christianity, the Church, and the Gospels were his constant subjects of irritation, fervor, or nostalgia? The paradox is only apparent. We must not forget his Christian upbringing: his prolonged and endlessly renewed readings of the scriptures; his love of the biblical style; the common, not merely puritanical, confusion among young bourgeois—and not only of his day—between sexual taboos and spirituality, whence his tireless polemic against orthodoxy as he imagined it and in which he (mistakenly) saw the sanction of a certain ethic; the conversion of some of his friends; and lastly, the piety of his wife. These biographical data do not constitute a character. They merely explain the *insistence* of the problem at the most diverse stages of Gide's development.

What really tormented him was ethics, not religion; justification, not salvation; what one experiences and how one judges, not pure knowledge or mystery. Did he reduce religion to morality? I prefer to think that morality was the locus of his true drama, and that he could approach religion only in this drama. Thus to become or become again a Christian could signify only sanctity for him, and not reception of the mystery, nor adherence to a creed. To have faith without being a saint seemed to him the essence of cheating, while he would have admitted sanctity without faith. Indeed, he expressly preferred it. But how define a saint who doesn't believe? A saint as lacking in faith as in religion, neither Christian nor Hindu, without mysticism or mystery? Would he not be an entirely banal man, reduced to a few ethical prejudices? But to pursue this subject would distract us from Gide's reality. An intense affectivity linked him, bound him to the world of Christianity, even if he refused its profoundest dimensions.

I have said that he mistrusted a certain "depth," which sometimes measures the distance between the ethical and the mystical, but which is often merely a bastard concept engendered by romanticism. Gide preferred to seek rectitude, which he held to be truth. He thus stopped at the exoteric logic of a sacred text, let us say at its merely ethical meaning. A typically Protestant inclination, or simply the consequence of a strict sobriety. His biblical erudition astounded me. The use he made of it I found disappointing. Where Claudel soars high, ricocheting symbols together, where Valéry would have politely declined, Gide raised objections, made deductions, worked himself up. Few writers, even Christian ones, have shown such love for the Gospels, and this even during the years when he doubted the existence of God.

But he believed in individual man, and this belief is a product of the synthesis of Christianity. It does not exist outside it, and cannot be explained without it. (Though I am not saying that it is Christian.) Gide was an individualist. Yet can we even now measure the scope and significance of this banality, one truly bizarre and unique in history, only one civilization out of the twenty-one we know of having made it possible and acceptable?

"Heretic among heretics," always eager to differ but also to legitimize his difference—no one could be more Occidental than Gide. No one could be less mystical in terms of traditional religion, in terms of myth, in terms of the stars and of the cosmic order, or in terms of the fatal and collective laws expounded by a party.

This is why the religious *problem*, as it is raised in the Christian world, and there alone, freed "by faith" from the empire of magic, has unceasingly occupied Gide's thought. And I do not know if this is good or bad: I am merely observing the existence of the phenomenon. I do not regard faith as a virtue any more than the absence of faith as a proof of courage. As for virtues and vices, in a given milieu, everyone is entitled to judge in the name of established norms. But faith and personal salvation have nothing to do with propriety, and are not in the scale of merits. And that is why it is written: "Judge not." I admit that I do not understand, or rather that I condemn such arguments about the belief or nonbelief of a famous man, multiplied and prolonged after his death nowadays. They derive from party spirit, which is the opposite of love of one's neighbor. They are neither Christian nor merely honest. "The Lord alone knows his own," say the scriptures: if one is Christian, one can believe that and leave to unbelievers the right to know better. And what good can such knowledge possibly do us? Except to serve as an argument and strangely reassure us in our faith or in our unbelief—because our side is strengthened by one more, and by one who is not the first-comer.

If Gide has totally refused anything, it is precisely totalitarianism, which is the logical development of party spirit. And first of all in religion. Will not tomorrow's true believer be the man who dares say: "I do not believe!" when the State invokes the necessities of history against him? There is no true faith without true doubt, any more than there is light without shadow. And I do not mean to say that Gide was a believer, but he remains an exemplary doubter.

AN EXTREME CASE

For my part, I had my doubts as to the validity of the conclusions I was entitled to draw from my conversations with Gide, concerning his private life, his judgments of himself, or his religious attitude. For instance: with regard to that surprising confession which I have carefully recounted, had the reading of *Love in the Western World* been only the pretext—or the real motivation? Had Gide merely yielded to that strange necessity (of which he so often complains) of entirely agreeing with his interlocutor—in order to recover himself immediately afterwards, alone with his *Journal?* Was he merely seeking the opportunity for an avowal which had long tempted him? Or had he really discovered a convincing "explanation" of his "errors"? How, at that moment, did he understand that last word? As a moralist who judged and condemned, or as a naturalist who observed himself?

Jean Delay's fascinating work *La Jeunesse d'André Gide* has permitted me to resolve some of these doubts. In the course of a conversation during the last days of his life (a good decade after our talks), Gide, writes Dr. Delay, "told me he attaches a very special importance" to *Love in the Western World* and to its analyses of the Tristan myth. "It is here," he added, "and not in the works of the psychoanalysts, that I have found the explanation of several of my errors, and of some of the earliest ones." [3] Starting from this point, Jean Delay reconstructs the Tristanian psychology so typical of *Les Cahiers d'André Walter* and of Gide's early "treatises," but whose persistence through his whole lifetime is attested by the posthumous fragments of the *Journal Intime* and of *Et Nunc Manet In Te*.

An invaluable confirmation, and one that has induced me to recapitulate in my turn, and in its entirety, the extreme case which Gide's life represents for me: an almost perfect example of dissociation of the person, permitting the coexistence—the simultaneous actuality—of two myths that normally exclude each other, of Tristan and Don Juan. [4]

[3] *La Jeunesse d'André Gide,* Volume I, 1956, p. 505.
[4] Note that Gide has never discussed any but the Greek myths (Prometheus, Theseus, Oedipus). Not a word about Tristan in his first works, and for Wagner "a passionate aversion." As for Don Juan, the character was certain to scandalize him. The action of our two myths in Gide's existence is therefore neither "literary" nor musical, as in Kierkegaard and Nietzsche. It is *not even conscious*. And that is what interests me.

From Gide's first book on, all the "notes" of Tristan are sounded.

Love is linked to the *separation* of the two lovers: André Walter's mother opposes his love for Emmanuèle; the latter marries a certain T., of whom we know nothing, and who is obviously present only to play the necessary role of King Mark. The extreme of separation being death, Emmanuèle must die, and André notes (in a sketch for a novel, anticipating reality): "a prodigous nirvana, in which the whole self is dissolved, annihilated in ecstasy, and still keeps the deliberate consciousness of its disappearance; this would be like a voluptuously perceptible nothingness." [5]

The beloved is ideal: she is "Beatrice," the eternal fiancée, "a chosen Lady, immaterially pure." She is, in fact, the Soul, and a soul conceived as "adversary" of the flesh. But the virtue of this word soul "is exhausted by repeating it: one must say *angel*." She is therefore the Angel, but at the same time the angel's "goal," "the angel's flight" to her lover. She is never a distinct, independent self, loved in her reality, but a disguised projection, the female double of André's self: "Veiled in black, at twilight, I have seen you leaning over the pillow of my bed, like a silent shadow. . . . I was afraid,

[5] Jean Delay, quoting this sentence, notes that it reveals the influence of Gide's reading of Schopenhauer. We know that this same reading was decisive for Wagner in writing *Tristan:* the nirvana André Walter invokes is Isolde's *höchste Lust*.

and the vision vanished." Elsewhere—and more than once—she is confused with the mother's image: "At evening I saw again *her* vanished profile in the shadow of your bent head . . . your voice when you talked made me remember. And soon my memory of you both grew confused, indistinct."

Because he is "afraid" of this recognition and of the double prohibition it implies, he cannot live with the woman he loves. Any excuse is good to avoid marriage or life together; and without external obstacles that would keep love from "turning to reality" (as the troubadours put it), he will provoke more secret ones. In his written work, his dream life, he will marry Emmanuèle to T. And in real life, everything will happen as the myth desires things to happen: the marriage which *nothing* opposes [6] is first postponed by odd scruples (which will be called puritanical for the simple reason that the engaged couple are Protestants); then, when it has been celebrated—too late, of course—it will never be consummated. The husband's travels and his wife's "delicate" health, his tastes and her silences—when a word could unravel everything!—the natural *données* and what appears to be the most spontaneous behavior, everything combines to save the law not of morality but of the myth: for it is forever inconceivable that Tristan and Iseult should marry, and if they do so nonetheless, it will be in appearance only. The special truth of their love forbids this reality.

[6] Delay, *op. cit.*, Volume II, 1957, p. 22.

Thus they will die as they have lived: separated from each other, and loving each other.[7]

Such is the mysterious complicity of contingent life and of the myth: mysterious in that it remains impossible to decide if it is the myth which has made life, or if life happened quite by accident to conform to the myth. Like Kierkegaard, Gide often complained of a "thorn in his flesh" which, he thought, unsuited him for marriage. Cause or effect of the myth's influence? The question, perhaps, has no meaning. One cannot help thinking that a piece of judicious advice, a few words said *in time* to this young man brought up in lunatic ignorance of the realities of the flesh, would have at least prevented the drama of the *mariage blanc*. But precisely—the myth exists, the myth is here, in this complicity of circumstances, in this conspiracy that resembles a destiny, and which as by magic avoids the advice and the accidents that would have opened the eyes of its willing victim.

NOMADISM, OR DON JUAN

"To leap to the other extreme of oneself" being one of Gide's most typical movements,[8] let us now consider, without transition, his Don Juan aspect.

It was during his honeymoon, experiencing the hide-

---

[7] *Et Nunc Manet In Te*, Éditions Ides et Calendes, 1951, pp. 12–13 and p. 7: "Last night, I was thinking of her; I was talking to her, as I often did, more easily in imagination than in her real presence; when suddenly I told myself: but she's dead!"

[8] *Si le Grain ne Meurt*, p. 251.

ous failure of his marriage, that Gide wrote his *Nourritures Terrestres*, a breviary of dionysian nomadism. Don
Juan appears, as though to avenge Tristan's inhuman
suffering. He disguises himself a little, to be sure of being
admitted. He first claims that his doctrine is justified by
Gide's religion: " 'The Gospels lead to it,' Euclid says;
'your doctrine shall be called Nomadism, from the beautiful word *nomos*, pasturage.' " [9] Later, he substitutes for
the term Nomadism, which might suggest infidelity—
and this is a Tristanian scruple—*disponibilité*, which has
the odor of charity, of generous accessibility, even of
love for one's neighbor. Indeed, what we find is the rejection of duration and the refusal to assume responsi-
bility for the other *person*, both characteristics of Don
Juan. "Gide doesn't stay in one place," Jean Paulhan
notes. "He prefers the hunt to the capture." The impatience of the adventurer, and of a certain type of sensualist. "The voluptuary Ménalque wants to forget the past
as he wants to be unaware of the future; he desires 'utter
oblivion of yesterday' and 'whatever future may come'
in order to surrender completely to the present moment,
to exult in it unrestrainedly, in a 'passionate stupefac-
tion.' " [10]

These voluptuous fantasies are the result of a tempera-
ment more excitable than well controlled: "For me . . .
who often, like Whitman, finds satisfaction in the most

[9] This was the epigraph for *Ménalque* when this central section
of the *Nourritures* appeared in periodical form. One of the first titles
Gide chose for *La Porte Étroite* was *Essai de Bien Mourir*. *Les Nourritures Terrestres* expresses the desire to oppose Don Juan's *here-and-
now* to Tristan's angelic *beyond*.

[10] Delay, *op. cit.*, Volume II, p. 598.

furtive contact," we read in *Si le Grain ne Meurt*. Swift gratifications without consequences, Don Juan's *presto* and perpetual flight! Here man and artist merge in the same impatience with "repetitions," for this is how Gide describes any liaison which implies a certain duration. (Moreover he has never stopped repeating it—but in different places.)

And here is the final, decisive characteristic: pure desire must be without love. (Hence pure love must be without desire.) In *Si le Grain ne Meurt*, in the pages where he describes his first sexual experience with a boy, he delightedly proclaims the very thing he will mourn in so many other pages of his works: "My joy was tremendous, and I could not have conceived its being any more complete had love been mingled with it. How could love have played any part? How could I have let desire dispose of my heart? My pleasure was without reservation and was to be followed by no remorse." [11]

It is this "tremendous joy" Gide wanted to talk about when he told me, in the conversation I have recounted, that he had been "shunted" that day, "onto a terribly wrong track."

THE DISSOCIATION OF LOVE AND DESIRE

To desire those you don't love, to love the woman you don't desire: this drama of the life of André Gide is that of an almost complete dissociation of the person, one that has made him a helpless victim of the tyranny

[11] *Si le Grain ne Meurt*, p. 346.

of the two myths—when one alone is quite enough for the misery of any man or for the passion of a fictional character.

To what degree can we hold Gide responsible for this "fundamental inability to combine mind and senses" [12] of which he was conscious so early? He has derived from it the best of his literary creation, has suffered it as a "thorn in the flesh"; it has ruined his private life, his marriage, and perhaps his wife's existence as well. At times he refers to it as a cruel fate, at times as his "quasi-mystical" choice, and at times, lastly, as a moral "error." In this fundamental perplexity, in this critical scrutiny which he occasionally brings to bear on his two dissociated *selves*—selves that enter into conflict with each other only by the action of this interrogation by virtually a Third Party—yes, in this Third Party excluded from his *amours* resides, no doubt, the true person of André Gide. [13]

In *Les Cahiers d'André Walter*, he feels and knows himself to be double: "Then I have so far disjoined them that I am no longer their master; each goes its own way, body and soul. The soul dreams of caresses ever more chaste; the body lets itself drift aimlessly. Wisdom, no doubt, deems they should be yoked together, that their pursuits should be made to converge. . . ." But is it

[12] *Si le Grain ne Meurt,* p. 173.

[13] ". . . and protecting in myself, simultaneously, the best and the worst, it is as a man drawn and quartered that I have lived. . . . The most contrary tendencies have never succeeded in making me a tormented being, only perplexed. . . . This *state of dialogue* . . . became necessary for me . . . it led me to the work of art. *Morceaux Choisis,* p. 434.

Gide *himself* who has disjoined them, so as no longer to
be their master—one becoming the prey of *Tristan,* the
other of *Don Juan?* Has he been the victim of the gods,
I mean of the myths? Or of an original error as to the
person? Or merely of his education and of puritan morality? The third hypothesis is the most likely at first
glance.

"My puritan upbringing had made a monster out of
the claims of the flesh." [14] Not only were they bad, they
were sinful. And in sin generally, there exists one sin
that is worse than any other—and which no one boasts
of having committed out of immoralist swagger. Now
the young Gide is touched by dread of this sin, if he
comes to desire a woman whom he *loves.* At the very
end of his life, speaking of his dreams, Gide remarks:
"but only in dreams, my wife's face is sometimes substi-
tuted, subtly and as though mystically, for my mother's,
without my being very surprised. The outlines of the
faces are not clear enough to keep my mind from shift-
ing back and forth between them . . . what's more: the
role one or the other plays in the dream's action remains
virtually the same, that is, an inhibitive role, which explains or motivates the substitution." [15]

---

[14] *Si le Grain ne Meurt,* p. 247.
[15] *Ainsi Soit-Il, ou les Jeux Sont Faits,* p. 128. The first words of
the quotation—"*only* in dreams"—are a curious example of repression.
Jean Delay quotes several sentences like the following (from Gide's
manuscript journal, January 1, 1886): "How many times, when Madeleine was in the next room, I confused her with my mother." Let us
recall that the two women were not at all alike, either physically or
morally. As for the last words—"*explains or motivates . . .*"—they

Brought up by women who were all, he tells us, "admirable Christian figures"—his mother, his governess, and two maternal aunts—"to whom the attribution of the slightest carnal awakening would have been an insult, it seemed to me"—then identifying his mother's image with that of his cousin Madeleine, whom he will nonetheless marry—how could Gide have overcome the prohibition thus cast upon his wife? Incapable of revoking the very *données* of this drama, seeking his salvation in flight, he resorts to Ulysses' method: "I'm not here. I'm nobody!" Before the imminence of the danger lurking so near the threshold of his consciousness, he cuts himself into two distinct beings: the monster will no longer find him! No longer know where to seek him out! I'm Tristan, look at my soul, it's an angel. I'm Don Juan, look at my body, that innocent animal. . . . Which is translated in moral terms by these two "rationalizations" (almost unconscious ones, of course, and which he will be the first to be surprised by when he finds the key to them much later): [16] 1) Loving his mother's image is permissible, as long as "carnal desire" is inhibited. 2) On the other hand, to desire the brown bodies of young "scamps" he will never see again is certainly not smiled upon in "our circles," but at least it does not violate the supreme prohibition.

indicate Gide's mistrust of the one-way causal relation posited by Freud—and by the entire nineteenth century.

[16] He notes, in *Ainsi Soit-Il*, p. 132: "I remember having already spoken elsewhere of this, which remains incomprehensible to me: that one can at the same time provide oneself all the elements of surprise, and be surprised. . . ."

Our immoralist's great audacity is typical of the half-measure, of the (actually vital) compromise between natural desire and an absolutely intransigent morality long anteceding Christianity and Victorian puritanism; further, sanctioned by the mother. Thus Gide "makes his decision to dissociate pleasure from love." And he even makes this necessity into a virtue: "It seemed to me that this divorce was desirable, that pleasure was thereby purer, love more perfect if the heart and the flesh were not involved with each other." [17] This is the means he found to respect both love and pleasure without violating the incest taboo and in somehow accommodating himself to the structures imposed upon his youth by maternal puritanism. A more "normal" Oedipus complex would perhaps have given Gide the aggressiveness necessary to break these puritan structures as, after all, countless young men brought up in the same tradition have done; but when his father died—a liberal and kindly man, many of whose character traits were less "virile," one might say, than his mother's, at least as Gide has described her—little André was almost eleven. His mother took him on her knees to console the sobbing child: "and suddenly I felt enveloped by that love, which henceforth closed over me." [18] The last words are not only touching. From this moment on, the die is cast, *les jeux sont faits*.

[17] *Si le Grain ne Meurt*, p. 289.
[18] *Ibid.*, p. 94.

I was about to say that Gide paid for this kind of security —the alternation of his dissociated *selves*—with his own person, quite literally. Yet however convenient the expression, it is false. It was Gide's *soul* that paid the price of his vital ruse.

We must agree, of course, on the definition of this word *soul*. I use it here in Nietzsche's signification, and in that of the mature Gide himself. According to the traditional conception of the Gnostics and even of Saint Paul, man consists of a physical body, a psychical body, a mental or spiritual body. For Nietzsche, the psychical is "the mortal soul . . . the soul as co-ordinator of the instincts and passions." For Gide, "a bundle of emotions, tendencies, susceptibilities, whose link is perhaps merely physiological." It is the seat of love in its various forms: love-as-desire, or love-as-gift ("The shift from one to the other always remains possible").[19] Gide distinguishes no further. "*Animus, Animum, Anima* . . . these discriminations make me dizzy." As we can see, moreover, when he writes somewhat later, speaking of his wife: "It was her soul I loved; and yet I didn't believe in that soul. I do not believe in the soul separated from the body." [20] (We understand that he no longer believed in a *distinct, personal spirit* which would be saved or destroyed after the death of the physical and animistic body, and which

[19] *Journal*, September 16, 1942.
[20] *Ibid.*, May 15, 1949.

our modern, even our religious terminology still confuses with the *soul*.)

This touching admission is one of the moments where Gide exists, "irreplaceable," where he rejoins his true *person*, because a Third Person in himself, which is his true ultimate self, finally assumes the insoluble conflict of his two souls. Meditating on these "extremes" so long cultivated, humored, isolated from each other—and which our two myths symbolize—I dare say in my turn, inverting Gide's admission and applying it to himself: it was his two souls that he had believed in, and his two souls no longer loved him. I refer here to the later Gide, fulfilled and balanced in his inner dialogue, as he describes himself in his *Morceaux Choisis*, published at fifty-two. His old age adds nothing which does not confirm such an image.

The man we may have known was neither Emmanuèle's paralyzed husband nor the nomad in pursuit of brief, sunbaked pleasures—neither André Walter nor Ménalque. It would have seemed quite incongruous to evoke, in the presence of this "inflexible Mongol with his scarab's head," [21] the alternate figures of Tristan and Don Juan. These two "extremes" whose "cohabitation" he had rejoiced at being able to protect seemed to have withdrawn from him, drawing with them his divided soul. As though evacuated from his person, they had become characters in his works. Yet in no one of these— save the *Journal*—have they ever "cohabited," whence the absence of profound tension which doubtless favored

[21] Jean Paulhan, in the *Nouvelle Revue Française* "Hommage."

their celebrated formal perfection and harmony at the expense of tragic power. By having been separately but *simultaneously* actualized, they had deprived Gide of that Shadow which is the inhibition of a potential part of the soul—hence its presence still, secret but active. These extremes no longer touched him. And too perfectly isolated from one another in his works, far from lending them a secret force, they spent their energy in the purity of a scrupulously alternate exercise.

There remained perplexity, serene or tormented, malicious or sulky, depending on the days or the interlocutor. Many minor problems of language or morality —but whose discussion often turned to hairsplitting—or else he gave in to you a little too quickly. Many *arrière-pensées* that he no longer wanted to follow up, and yet it was these that made him still so engaging, and sometimes touching, for those who loved his books. In short, despite his still lively curiosity and his generosity, an almost instinctive refusal to deepen and enlarge, to integrate and extend, coupled with an increasingly marked propensity to seek the contrary of all this—that is, to bound and limit, to dissociate and demystify. This attitude has its virtue, which is that of doubt. But it also reveals what I must call—"now that I see more clearly"—a certain desiccation of the soul and of its expansive powers.

This accounts for that impression I had kept of him, and which I interpreted as a lack of spiritual imagination —for me the true poetic sense. (He preferred to speak of his "refusal to entertain" any kind of reality inaccessible to the "rational.") I distinguish more clearly today the functional origins of this flight of the divided soul, and how it ultimately, inevitably occurred in the development of his person.

Was Gide the victim of the end of an era already cruel and absurd in our eyes, as the conflicts provoked in the life of an Aztec by the decrees of mad, dead gods may appear absurd or simply uninteresting? Or was he rather an actor sacrificed to his role in the soul's drama, an actor who will live as long as our West and its myths? Nietzsche boasted of having written the only work in the world ending in *or else?*—Gide joins him here, but by his life.

THE PERSON, THE ANGEL,
AND THE ABSOLUTE

or, the East-West Dialogue

AN ILL-STARRED DIALOGUE

THE West discovers Zen just as the Zen monasteries are emptying in Japan; but there are many more Japanese Christians than followers of Doctor Suzuki in America. The West discovers Hindu wisdom through the somewhat Christianized presentations of Ramakrishna's successors; but the intelligentsia of India is already preoccupied with problems imposed on it by Western technology and hygiene, and is attempting to solve them by a socialism that owes nothing to Shankara. The West discovers Zoroaster in Nietzsche's wake and publishes the major texts of the Sufi mystics; but Iran and Arabia are adapting themselves to the capitalist *habitus*. The West discovers and publishes the *I Ching*; but China is industrializing itself, adopting Marxism, and obliterating its own mandarinate. Finally, the West discovers Negro art, masks, magic, and jazz; but Africa races toward nationalism, parliamentary government, and exploitation of its own natural resources.

What enthralls us about Asia and Africa is not what they have lived on, but what is missing in our own elite, or what it can no longer find in our own faith. What Africa and Asia borrow from us is not our creativity, but its products.

We discover their spiritual secrets at the same time as the poverty which was their price. They adopt our social forms, our governmental procedures, and our technology, but not the spiritual tensions which were their secret motivation. What for us was the consequence of countless impulses and resistances, laboriously balanced, slowly assimilated, becomes for them sudden turmoil.

In such a situation, what can intellectuals and religious thinkers do? Almost nothing, except to state essentials, which will scarcely influence history in the immediate future, but may affect the minds of those who will make it tomorrow.

The essentials of the necessary and henceforth inevitable dialogue, however ill-starred its beginnings, concern man and his definition. If it is true that the East denies the *self*, which is a central value for the West, the result is a series of infinite consequences in all the domains of reality, from the spiritual to the political; yet how true *is* such a statement? Which is the self that affirms its being, on the one hand, and which is the self that is denied, on the other? Are they one and the same?

THE PERSON

Christianity has formed the West by forming, from the first Councils, its models of thought in tension: Incarnation, divine persons both linked and distinct. Whence the definition of the human person or of the *true self*, revived and redefined by all the great periods of theology and of philosophy, and always opposed to the *natural man*, a more or less rational animal and simple specimen of the race.

For Saint Paul, the true self is the *new man*, "called"

by a personal God, hence created by a vocation; he does not fall under the yoke of the senses like the "old Adam," since the "new" life is both in and out of the world, manifested by his love (Agapè) and "hidden with Christ in God" (Colossians, 3:3).

In the Greek Fathers and in the Latin Boethius, through Joannes Scotus Erigena, down to Hugh of Saint Victor, and later in Thomism, we can follow the development of the concept and the term *person*, forged by Trinitarian doctrine: more and more frequently it will be applied to the new man, to the *ens sibi* which the spirit raises in the natural individual. For Descartes, the true self is the "soul," but he means an entirely intellectual soul, whose "nature is only to think" and which remains entirely distinct from the body. With Kant, the true, noumenal self is opposed to the phenomenal self, and again takes the name *person*. In Renouvier, the person appears as a "function with several variables," thereby endowed with a freedom inaccessible to the individual, that single object of universal determinism. And as for today's science, which is sometimes said to "approach the self only to disintegrate it," [1] it seems to me that it only prunes the true self, disintegrating what belongs only to

[1] Cf. Charles Baudoin: *Découverte de la Personne*, 1940, p. 22. (This work is the best exposition of modern personalism by a psychoanalyst whose views are close to those of C. G. Jung.) But if Baudoin seems to me a little too pessimistic, D. T. Suzuki goes too far in the other direction when he writes with obvious satisfaction: "Modern psychology has in fact done away with an ego-entity." (*Mysticism: Christian and Buddhist* [New York, Harper & Row, 1957], p. 39.) The psychology to which he refers is Western. Seeking to cure the "sicknesses of the self," it confirms that self as an entity and reinforces rather than eliminates it.

the collective (unconscious, overself, archetypes) or to
the biological (heredity, endocrine balance), and pre-
sents it as all the more *distinct*, in its central, integrating
function, its power to unify being. Far from dissociating
the self, the psychological researches of the twentieth
century name and reveal those forces tending to dissociate it, the neuroses assailing it on all sides, and recover,
by the detour of their "objective" descriptions, the Pauline opposition of the "two men in me": the tyrannizing
natural man (tyrannized in turn by the law) and the
liberating spiritual man.

If it is true that in common speech we rarely trouble
to distinguish the *person* from all it is not—individual,
persona, "strong individuality," sensitive soul, intellect,
even an elementary and often deceptive self-conscious-
ness—the fact remains that belief in a distinct self and
recourse to an "absolute value of the person" are virtually universal in the West. As is attested by so many
concepts regarded as self-evident—and so many realities
"approved" in the West—but which the East persists in
ignoring, even condemning, such as originality, the
rights of man, the record, personal glory, biography,
portraiture, prayer for a living individual or for the
dead. As is also attested, in the West, by the bad connota-
tion of anonymity, by our critical condemnation of an
impersonal style or of banality, by our philosophical denunciation of "one" as a subject, by our Marxist diatribes
against alienation. As is attested, lastly, by our notion
of love—to which I shall return below.

194

THE ANGEL

What is this portion of the person henceforth liberated from the world where it still lives in exile, but "an heir of the Kingdom," henceforth "bearing the celestial image," "glorified," "clad" in light, incorruptibility, and immortality; henceforth, then, "risen with Christ," although "hidden with Christ in God" until the advent of Love?

It is the Angel, answers the Iran of Mazdaism, the Iran of the Sufi mystics, close to India but grafted onto the Abrahamic stock, from which have issued the Jews, the Christians, and Islam.

What is the Angel to our psychologists? A projection of the individual or collective self. For the sages of Iran, it *is* that self. Barakat, a Jew converted to Islam, writes in 1165: "for each individual soul, or perhaps for several having the same nature or affinity, there is a spiritual being which throughout their existence assumes toward this soul or this group of souls a special solicitude and tenderness; this being initiates them into knowledge, protects them, guides them, comforts them, leads them to victory, and this being is called *Perfect Nature*." This is the true self, this is the Angel. "No longer merely a messenger transmitting orders, nor the common idea of the guardian Angel . . . the form in which each of the mystics knows God is also the form in which God knows him, because it is the form in which God is revealed to Himself in him. . . . It is the 'share allotted' to each mystic, his absolute individuality, the Divine Name invested in him." [2] Thus, according to Henry Corbin's admirable commentaries on the Sufi mystics, "the totality of our being is not only that portion we now call our person, for this totality also includes another person, a transcendent counterpart which remains invisible to us, what Ibn'Arabî calls our 'eternal individuality,' our 'Divine Name,' what ancient Iran called *Fravarti*." [3]

The Angel of the Sufis designates not only this initiating share of the regenerate being that remains hidden in God according to Christianity, but further, and more precisely with regard to its homology, those celestial *feminine* entities which the religion of Zarathustra called the *Fravartis*, "those who have chosen" (that is, chosen to fight on the side of Ormazd) and who are both the celestial archetypes of beings and their tutelary angels. Further: according to Mazdaism "each physical or moral entity, each complete being or each group of beings belonging to the world of Light has its Fravarti"—even Ormazd, the god of light, has his own.[4] The physical earth and all the beings which inhabit it thus appear as the visible counterpart of the invisible but primordial world of the archetypes.

The major event, the crucial scene of the drama of the

[2] Henry Corbin, *L'Imagination Créatrice dans le Soufisme d'Ibn'-Arabi*, 1958, pp. 28 and 50.

[3] *Ibid.*, p. 131.

[4] Henry Corbin, *Terre Céleste et Corps de Résurrection*, 1960, p. 31.

person thus constituted takes place at the dawn of the third night after the terrestrial death: it is the meeting of the soul with its celestial self at the entrance to the Shinvat Bridge. In a landscape haloed with the Light-of-Glory restoring all things and all beings to their paradisiac purity, "in a setting of mountains gleaming with the light of dawn, celestial waters in which the plants of immortality grow," in the center of the spiritual world (which is the real world of the archetypes), the Shinvat Bridge springs forth, linking one summit to the world of infinite Lights. At its gate the soul meets its *Daena*, its celestial self, a young woman of resplendent beauty, who says to it: *"I am thyself!"* But if a man has mistreated his soul on earth, it is a monstrous and disfigured apparition, instead of the Fravarti, that reflects his fallen state. The "dawn meeting" with the celestial self thus represents a weighing of souls.

Mazdaism, like the Sufis later, and like Christianity, does not ask first *what is* man, but who *are you?* All ultimate reality is personal. The true self is elsewhere, but its drama here on earth.

THE ABSOLUTE, OR THE NEGATION
OF THE SELF

The peoples of the regions Europe calls Asia differ much more among themselves than the peoples of Europe, yet if there is one belief they all share, it is the belief in metempsychosis, the transmigration of souls. Now this

belief seems at first glance to imply quite necessarily the
belief in a self recognizable through its successive lives.
For if the self does not exist, what is it that transmi-
grates? [5] But this self, this ego, this distinct entity, is precisely what the doctrines of India, or those produced in
India like Buddhism, have denounced for thousands of
years as the fundamental illusion. Is there then a rift between the people and their sages, between the religion of
the former and the metaphysics of the latter? As a matter of fact, we do not find the sages of Asia unremittingly
denouncing, as we might have expected, the popular beliefs of their countries; it is much more *our* notion of the
person that they oppose with their concept of the nonself. Has the real rift yawned between them and ourselves? Between what they think we believe when we
affirm the real self, and what we think they believe when
they deny it?

We may make some progress by trying to determine
what their negations were directed against, in those early
times when our affirmations did not exist or remained
unknown to them.

In the first commentaries on the Vedas, it appears that
the negation of the self first refers to the natural man,
the transitory and "blind" animal, the obscuring en-
velope of a divine soul. This is how all the Upanishads
put the matter, as do the first canonical writings of Buddhism: man must extinguish individual desire, the cause
of error, suffering, and death, must dissipate this screen

---

[5] On the solutions proposed by India, Taoism, and Tibetan Buddhism, see Alexandra David-Neel: *Immortalité et Réincarnation*, 1961.

of matter between reality and the soul. One might assume that this is the same "death to the world and to oneself" which Christ asks of his disciples and which is the condition of their accession to their true spiritual self, the one which will rise in a transfigured body. Vedantists, Vishnuites, and Shivaites admit an individual soul (the *jîva*), but it is "obscured" by its union with the body. It must seek to free itself from the individual phenomenon, whereas the Christian soul must transfigure it —whence the "resurrection of the flesh."

The same is true of Buddhism in its earliest form. What is man? A transitory combination of material aggregates and mental formations subject to selfish desire, which is born of ignorance and inevitably involves attachments to illusion; whence action, process, death, and the wheel of endless return. "Unknowable is the beginning of the beings enveloped by ignorance, and whom desire leads to criminal rebirths." [6] The goal is thus "to teach us the means not to be reborn," as a modern interpreter of Tibetan Buddhism tells us.[7] At the other geographical (and sometimes spiritual) end of the continent, an interpreter of Zen echoes this observation: "The denial of *Atman* as maintained by earlier Buddhists refers to *Atman* as the relative ego and not to the absolute ego, the ego after enlightenment-experience." [8] Or in the Sanskrit of the Buddha:

[6] Statement attributed to Buddha, in the tradition of the Theravadins (Hinayanists).

[7] Cf. Alexandra David-Neel, *Le Bouddhisme du Bouddha*, 1960, pp. 51–59.

[8] D. T. Suzuki, *Mysticism: Christian and Buddhist*, p. 47.

199

Sabbe sankhāra anicca
Sabbe sankhāra dukkha
Sabbe dhamma anatta

(All created things are transitory
All created things are sorrowful
All the elements of being are nonself) [9]

If D. T. Suzuki can write, after this: "As we see, personal experience is the basis of Buddhist philosophy," we must realize that he is referring to a rigorously spiritual experience. In the end, the chief adversary of the Vedantists, as of the first Buddhists, is not yet the person, but the persistence of the ego that wants to survive death without understanding anything of the conditions of this survival, without first purifying its *jīva*—without first disciplining itself, we would say, to the requirements of the true self, which is our celestial counterpart. And this reputedly illusory self must exist and must be strong if one of the major goals of the spiritual discipline is to keep it from being reborn! [10]

[9] *The Dhamma Pada*, Radakrishnan translation.
[10] David-Neel gives a Tibetan parable of the "person" in *Le Bouddhisme du Bouddha:*

"'A person' is like an assembly composed of a number of members. The discussion never ends. Sometimes one of its members stands up, makes a speech, advises an action; his colleagues approve of what he says and it is agreed that what he has proposed will be carried out. At other times, several members of the assembly stand up at the same time, propose different things, each of them basing his proposals on separate reasoning. The members reach the point of challenging and fighting each other.

"It also happens that certain members of the assembly leave it of their own accord; others are gradually removed and still others are forcefully expelled by their colleagues. During this time, newcomers are introduced into the assembly, either slipping in unnoticed or beating down the doors.

"Moreover certain members of the assembly die off slowly; their

But then comes the second stage, in which the religious writers even oppose the absolute ego, the reality of the distinct soul. The individual self is identified with the Self of the Immensity, or of Brahma. What is the soul? A monad, according to some. A reflection of Brahma, according to others. No, the Advaitins reply: there is only *brahman.* And *you* are nothing. And in their turn, the Buddhists (but the Chinese Tao and the Japanese Shinto say the same thing in virtually the same phrases):

> "Nagasena, does there exist a being that transmigrates from this body into another?"
> "No, there is no such thing."
> "If there is no transmigration, can there be a reincarnation?"
> "Yes, it is possible."

Here is the explanation:

> "Nagasena, is there someone who does not resume his individuality after death?"
> "He who has sinned resumes his individuality, but a pure being does not."

voices weaken until they are no longer heard. On the contrary, others who were weak and timid grow stronger and bolder, and finally establish themselves as dictators.

"The members of this assembly are the physical and mental elements constituting the 'person'; they are our instincts, our tendencies, our ideas, our beliefs, our desires, etc. Each of these happens to be, by the causes which have engendered it, the heir and descendant of many causes, many series of phenomena going far back into the past and whose traces are lost in the depths of eternity."

This image is familiar enough in the West. Bismarck writes: "Faust complained of having two souls in his breast. I have a host of turbulent souls in myself. And everything happens as in a Republic."

By considering the self this way, one assuredly and methodically loses it. If one tried to observe an elephant with a microscope, the elephant too would be no more than a tremendous illusion.

"O Nagasena, tell me if there exists anything like
unto the soul?"

"There is no thing like unto the soul." [11]

A Chinese Zen text goes further:

"Is there a teaching to give the people?"

"Yes."

"What is it?"

"There is neither spirit, nor Buddha, nor anything
which exists." [But of course this lesson is never
given to the people. Far from it!]

The Hindu mystics seek *samādhi*, which is total ab-
sorption in the Absolute of the Self: the great sleep,
slowly attained, and which one might call *enstasis*. And
the Christian mystics seek *ecstasis*. As for the Zen Buddhists, it is as if they kept to *stasis* pure and simple: confront the fact, sign of the Whole, and thus of the Void.
Their *satori* is the contrary of *samādhi*: it is an instantaneous awakening. Awakening of what? Of vision-in-
itself, of the *that* which is not personal and which functions through our self.

So much for the Orient of doctrines. And at the same
time the Orient of the people and their belief in transmigration. But this is the moment to adjust our vision. The
entire Orient exaggerates its formulas. It says a *hundred
thousand million* when it means *many; absolute negation*
when it means *caution; immortality* when it means *lon-
gevity*. Our Western hygiene, increasing the average
length of life by fifty years, would thus be a "recipe for

[11] *The Questions of Milinda (Milindapanha)*, first century A.D.
Milinda is the Indo-Greek king Menander, who lived in the second
century B.C. Nagasena is a Buddhist Patriarch.

immortality." Indeed the only one that has succeeded. Let us therefore learn to see through their lenses.

The same Kitaro Nishida who writes: "Religious value signifies the absolute negation of the self," adds three pages farther: "We become true persons insofar as we confront the all-transcendent *One*." [12] (Which is Christian.)

The same Chang Chen-Chi who quotes this *koan:*

Sometimes I abolish the person but save the object.
Sometimes I abolish the object but save the person.
Sometimes I abolish both object and person together.
Sometimes I abolish neither object nor person.

comments:

To abolish the person and save the object signifies: to eliminate the questioner, not his question. And the other three distinctions can be explained in the same manner.

Then he adds:

If the disciple is exceptionally endowed, the master touches neither the person nor the object.

And finally this:

As Bodhidharma [the founder of Zen] has declared, Zen is not concerned to discourse on abstruse notions such as God or the Truth; what Zen asks of the disciple is to *see his own physiognomy*.

Or, as the Sixth Patriarch of the sect (638–713) said:

[12] K. Nishida, *Die Intelligible Welt*, pp. 116 and 119.

Think of neither good nor evil, but contemplate your *original physiognomy* at the present moment—the one you had even before being born.[13]

Which brings us back to one version of Christianity—having started from one version of Buddhism—and certainly to Mazdaism and the Sufis: we are concerned with a single spiritual quest whose Grail, or Angel, is: *thyself*.

Thus the differences are not what they were presumed, are never exactly what they were presumed. If we want to determine their nature, we are likely to find out most by examining the notions of love that translate these three conceptions. In this realm, every acknowledged difference can be verified by inner experience, and affords the dialogue of the mystics a broadening of the consciousness which each will gain from his own. Whereas on the level of today's more or less "scientific" anthropology, it would seem that the Oriental negations of the self simply correspond to the neuroses of Freudian psychoanalysis: so many "rationalizations" of "dysfunctional" attitudes which threaten the self's integrity and which deny or destroy the person. But the Oriental smiles and leaves us "our" problems.

THREE SCHOOLS OF LOVE

If love is the prime mover not only of man but of the world, it is love's action which configures our idea of

[13] David-Neel, *Le Bouddhisme du Bouddha*, pp. 304–305.

the self, and this idea of the self reveals love, as the structure of the atom reveals certain properties of energy. "It is the prevailing love which makes man. . . . Man is no more nor less than the prevailing love of his life: according to this love is made his heaven, if he is good, or his hell, if he is bad," Swedenborg says in *The New Jerusalem*. And in *De Coelo* he adds: "The body of each spirit and of each angel *is* the form of its love." [14]

The three notions of man we have evoked above seem, then, so many models of an energetics of love, or so many effects of its configuring and creative action. And we find them differing in a subtle but precise manner by the form of the relations they posit between the *natural self* and the *true self*—that is, depending on the languages, between phenomena and noumena, between individual and person, between soul and angel, between ego and self.

Let us note that all three start from a duality without which neither man nor love would be even conceivable. I am not referring here to either the dualism so facilely called Manichean, opposing good and evil as two pre-existing principles; nor to the "two men within me," whose struggle made Saint Paul groan aloud; but, preceding any moral judgment, to a bipolarity, a permanent tension between the individual and the "true self." (The individual is not evil in himself: he becomes bad only insofar as he closes himself, refuses himself to love. Simi-

[14] These two sentences should be compared with a Sufi view: "The paradise of the faithful Gnostic is his own body, and the hell of the man with neither faith nor knowledge is also his own body." (Quoted by Corbin, *Terre Céleste*, p. 161.)

larly the "true self" is not good in itself, for it can become a monster.)

To love, we must be two, says the wisdom of nations. And it applies first of all to the love of ourself, without which there is no love for our "neighbor."

The world's moralists agree with the mystics in their condemnation of egoism, which is the imperialism of the natural ego and its autarchic closing-up. But the motives for this condemnation are not the same: the moralists judge in the name of society, the mystics in the name of love. We shall invoke only the second group here.

THE CHRISTIAN SCHOOL

In the Christian view of man, love of oneself is the positive relation between the individual and the true self. The second commandment, which summarizes all the Law and the Prophets: "Love thy neighbor *as* thyself," obviously supposes a *dual* self, at the heart of which love is established so that loving oneself and loving one's neighbor is one and the same act: if not, the *as* would not have its full meaning. In the love of oneself, the natural man opens himself to the action of the true, spiritual self and lets himself be transformed, reoriented by it. It is the true self that loves, that is the agent of love. Only this true self can love its neighbor, for only the self discerns the same love in another. "To love is to sustain, to divine, to bear the best of what one loves" as Alain says. Now the best in another person—as in oneself—is his singular vocation. To love one's neighbor in his person is to discern his singularity, his vocation, even when it is virtual—to sustain and help it to be born. Hence love, in its total reality, integrating the animistic and the spiritual, always proceeds from person to person.

But then, where does the person come from? Whatever the name given it by the three Abrahamic religions, the true self is always brought into being by love itself: "God has loved us first." For the Christian, it is because God, who is Love, is a personal God in his tri-unity, because spiritual love creates the person in man.

If the highest value of the Christian West is not the knowledge of detachment but personal sacrifice, and if sacrifice differs from suicide—only the nature of true love explains this. "Greater love hath no man than this, that a man lay down his life for his friends." To sacrifice oneself for the beloved other person is first of all to sacrifice one's *self* to one's *true self*—to accept one's vocation. Or further: it is to sacrifice oneself *as one is* to oneself *as one is to become* by the action of spirit. It is to rejoin the immortal form of one's being through a transfiguring "death to oneself."

The model of love and of the true self establishes the normal, the sublime, and the problematical for the Christian West. It also conditions love's deviations and the particular forms which certain morbid tendencies will take in the West—tendencies perhaps universal but here so highly specified that it is sometimes impossible to recognize their homologues elsewhere. Let us consider two extreme examples.

RELIGIOUS MASOCHISM, OR SELF-HATRED. In his dramatic language, Saint Paul sometimes speaks of the hatred of oneself, a formulation taken literally and used with mounting satisfaction by all religious writers of an ascetic tendency. I am well aware that hatred is love's obverse, yet how can love, fascinated by desire for what is its object, truly hate what it sacrifices to that object? Is not masochism the moment of the frustrated soul's *relapse*, when the spirit which invoked it ceases to direct its impulse toward the true self? The soul desired the Angel. It is left with the nostalgia of a flight beyond the natural self. Henceforth the Old Adam is judged: the soul, unable to take the Old Adam along toward its goal and to animate him with its love, accuses him of bad will. Yet it knows that they are bound together, and that the soul itself will die if it kills the Old Adam. It then contents itself with cursing the Old Adam, calling him "the body of this death," and their relations grow infected. Most so-called "sexual" neuroses have their genesis in this permanent discord—in the soul's rejection of the body taken as the sign and symbol of the self's "prison." And this is because the soul had dreamed of an angelic metamorphosis, when all that spirit asked was the submission of the entire terrestrial and temporal self to the vocation of love. But anyone who hates himself in this way cannot love his neighbor: he can see him only in his own image—a "vile" body and a soul aspiring to be an angel—not the true self in its autonomy. If the body seems desirable to him, he will occasionally be tempted to attribute this instinctual impulse to the revelation of an angelic love. This is the source of romantic passion. Exalted to the mystique of self-punishing *ascesis*, it ultimately confuses the death instinct with the necessary death of the pseudo-self.

Against this nontransfiguring asceticism, Nietzsche writes with some reason: "We must beware the man who hates himself, for we are sure to be the victims of his anger and his vengeance. Let us therefore try to persuade him to love himself." [15]

SENSUAL EROTICISM is the other extreme to which the soul attains, irritated but not converted by spirit—as Kierkegaard has so well observed. All true love proceeds from the true self and is directed toward the other person's true self. But it may stop on the way, its impulse toward the singular person may lapse to the level of the individual, the generic. Tapped by the instinct which it arouses beyond natural requirements, it will fatally exhaust itself in the illusory multiplicity of "inconsequential adventures."

Limiting its desire to those *desires* which rapid possession anesthetizes, the soul then lapses into the bonds of instinct, which is the impersonal power par excellence, and futilely struggles to free itself by varying the excitation, by perpetual rejection of attachments. This is the

[15] *The Dawn,* § 517.

negative freedom claimed by Don Juan against the
conventions of everyday morality—which he is already
too "spiritual" to respect—but also against the respect
for the demanding mystery of the Other Person—whom
he is not "spiritual" enough to love. (But if he were,
he would also recover the justification of certain conventions, protecting the spirit's earliest fortunes in the
primitive and the innocent—or sheltering from the
spirit's onslaught the indispensable connective tissue of
all societies which are not an *order*.)

THE IRANIAN SCHOOL

There no longer exists a human community, a unit of
civilization which takes its inspiration from Zarathustra's
Mazdaism; and none will ever again be inspired by the
mysticism of the Sufis, and with reason. If I invoke
them here, it is as an evocation of a virtual, nontemporal,
and hence permanent spiritual dimension: Mazdaism and
the Sufis have proposed notions of men and love
homologous to the Christian notions, but as though
transposed one degree toward the "heaven" of the archetypes: thus the duality of ego versus true self here
becomes that of the soul and its Angel.

To situate the essential personalism of these doctrines
in its true spiritual climate,[16] let us quote this verse of
the Koran (24-41) as a kind of musical key signature:

[16] On this point see the splendid essays of Hans Heinrich Schaeder
collected in *Der Mensch in Orient und Okzident,* 1960, particularly:
"Das Individuum in Islam."

"Each being knows the mode of prayer and of glorification that is proper to it." Each person originates in God, who has created him in order to be known by and to become in that person the object of His own knowledge. It is therefore in God that love can recognize the neighbor's person and love it "as himself"—as born of the same love that created me. "(God) is the one who in each loved being is manifested to the regard of each lover . . . for it is impossible to love a being without representing to oneself the divinity within him. . . . A being actually loves none other than his creator." [17]

Ibn'Arabī distinguishes three kinds of love: the *divine love* of the Creator for his creature, and of the creature for Him; the *spiritual love* "whose seat is in the creature forever seeking the Being whose Image it discovers within itself, or whose Image it discovers itself to be"; lastly the *natural love* which seeks the satisfaction of its desires without concern for the pleasure of the Beloved. "And this, alas!" says Ibn'Arabī, "is the way most people today understand love."

How reconcile natural love (or physical love, as it is improperly called) with spiritual love? *Who* loves in us, and *for whom?* "Ibn'Arabī observes that the most perfect mystical lovers are those who love God simultaneously *for himself* and *for themselves*, because this capacity reveals in them the unification of their double nature (the denouement of the 'stricken consciousness' struggling with its lacerations)." Such then is the unified

---

[17] Ibn'Arabī, in Corbin, *L'Imagination Créatrice dans le Soufisme d'Ibn'Arabī*, p. 111.

person and such is his love for himself. As for love-as-passion (here nonromantic!), it is situated at the point where the soul's gaze suddenly recognizes in the Beloved that visible form of the divine, that theophany the soul can love in all the dimensions of unified love.

The Beloved is then no longer a simple object—as in natural, possessive love—but a divine virtuality which the lover "imagines" (whose image he divines) and which he brings into being in the Beloved by the effectiveness of his prefiguring love.

> It is precisely at this point that the highest function of human love originates, the very one that assures the coalescence of what we have historically designated as courtly love and mystical love. For love tends to the transfiguration of the beloved earthly figure, by surrounding it with a light showing forth all its superhuman virtualities, even investing it with the theophanic function of the Angel [as with the feminine figures celebrated by the *Fedeli d'amore*, Dante's associates; as with the Female Figure that appeared to Ibn'Arabī, at Mecca, as the face of the divine Sophia]. The lover tends to contemplate the beloved being, to unite himself with it, to perpetuate its presence; his love always tends to bring into being something not yet existent in the Beloved.[18]

Here we recognize the "notes" of Kierkegaard's love-of-one's-neighbor,[19] but also Swedenborg's:

> As all goods proceed from the Lord, the Lord is, in the highest sense and in a supereminent degree, the Neighbor from whom the source of Neighbor is derived;

[18] *Ibid.*, p. 117.
[19] Cf. *supra*, pp. 127–29.

consequently the degree in which anyone is a neighbor is according to how much of the Lord he has with him; and because no one receives the Lord, that is, receives good from Him, in quite the same way as another, therefore no one is a neighbor in quite the same way as another. . . . There is never identically the same good with any two people. . . . It is love that makes a neighbor of anyone, and everyone is neighbor according to the quality of his love.[20]

Despite everything that distinguishes the (occasionally deceptive) transparency of the engineer-philosopher Swedenborg from the dense poetry of the Arab, the analogy of these statements is undeniable. If the concrete symbolism of the Sufis doubly transposes every term in both the supernatural (or heavenly world) and in the earthly world of the senses, the structure of the relations between God, the true self, and the neighbor remains exactly comparable, as do the three forms of love which this structure manifests. But how much more vividly the "creative imagination" of the Sufis, like the angelology of Mazdaism, makes us *see* the primary and final unity of all love!

Perhaps, too, it will let us glimpse how the Tristan myth—despite the pseudo-Buddhism Wagner tardily borrowed from Schopenhauer—participates in the Iranian spiritual climate and finds its archetypal origins there. The hero's passion, which can be interpreted (in the primitive legend and the opera) as a love dedicated

---

[20] Emmanuel Swedenborg: *The New Jerusalem and Its Heavenly Doctrine,* §§ 86–89.

to his own soul,[21] of which Isolde would be merely the perceptible *image*—and this is why I have gone so far as to say that Tristan did not love Isolde—is not this passion *seen* more clearly if we evoke the Fravarti of Mazdaism, the angelic figures of the true self in Sufi mysticism, and even the "dawn meetings" of the soul and its Daena on the Shinvat Bridge? And is it not because they desired an angelic love that the lovers of the Forest of Morrois discover that their passion demands their separation, for "their engagement," as Novalis will say—"was not made for this life," but for the other? If there is an "*erreur de Tristan*," motivating the essential misfortune of his passion, it would then be in the *mode of transposing* "Heaven" to earth, Angel to woman, that we might foresee its ultimate secret. (Here, then, all everyday or rational morality that is not strictly personalist can obviously only decline judgment.)

THE ORIENTAL SCHOOL

Most of the Hindu doctrines, and all of the Buddhist schools, as we have seen, deny or pass over the person, acknowledging only the transitory ego and the impersonal Self: "*There is only one Self for all beings.*" [22] The individuality apparent to the senses must be me-

---

[21] This is virtually what Freud calls "narcissism," and which is such only in the eyes of the man who denies the soul; but then, where would this love come from, to whom would it go? Tristan's passion is the proof of the soul, if there ever was one.

[22] *Katha Upanishad.*

thodically *extenuated* (not transfigured or glorified) in order to achieve the Self without distinction, the Reality without countenance, which is neither one nor the other, but which is Immensity, say the Hindus, and which is Void, say the Buddhists.

The problems of loving oneself, loving God, and loving one's neighbor are thereby got rid of at one blow: without real protagonists, these problems could not take place (or at least be taken seriously). Love itself is got rid of. It is nothing more than the attraction of the sexes inevitably functioning in the millions and millions of ephemeral aggregates, combined and undone according to the course of the planets and Karma. For spirit, there can be only indifference. (Although social morality radically condemns the adultery of the married woman; but not in the name of love, of course.)

"Abandon things, O lover, your way is flight!" exclaims Saint John of the Cross. "Abandon the neighbor!" add the mystics of Vedantism and Buddhism. If it is true that the "notion of the Self is admitted only to the minds of fools," as one Tibetan text puts it, the notion of a Thou is not worth much more. "Buddhist morality, which is a kind of spiritual hygiene, tends to destroy our reasons for suffering in behalf of someone else." [23] "The nature of ultimate reality can be grasped only after having destroyed all innate or acquired attachment to one's kind. . . ." [24] And Buddha himself: "He who has a hundred kinds of love has a hundred kinds of sorrow;

---

[23] David-Neel, *Le Bouddhisme du Bouddha*, p. 45.
[24] Chang Chen-chi, *The Practice of Zen.*

he who has one love has one sorrow; he who has no love has no sorrow."

If we consider only the texts, we can see why: metaphysical Asia knows nothing of love—I mean the love of God, of oneself, and of one's neighbor, love-as-passion, and even matrimonial love.

It may be objected that Asia is not only metaphysical, and that life does not consider only the texts. It may be added that there is no reason why the actual Orient should conform more closely to Buddha's sermons than Europe to the Sermon on the Mount. Such objections are incorrect.

For the great religious doctrines of Asia have never been revolutionary. They have never claimed to transform the whole of human reality: social, economic, political, or even moral. On the one hand (as religions), they express these realities, they establish and consecrate them (by the idols and the *yantras*—magic and invariable signs—by the daily omnipresent rites, by the caste system and the condemnation of all curiosity about the world); on the other, as doctrines they offer the mystic a means of escaping the world by upsetting matters as little as possible. The Abrahamic religions, on the contrary, both monotheist and communitary, *attack* the whole of human relations and take to task each individual in his present state, resolved to *transform* him.[25] They provoke countless reactions. Hence it is inevitable that

[25] All this applies to Islam, of course, at least as much as to Christianity and Judaism. "For the Arab, everything is anger," writes Henri Michaux. "His greeting: 'Salvation to the follower of the *true* religion.' (The true one! To the rest, no greeting.)" (*A Barbarian in Asia.*)

216

actual life, in the West, resembles doctrine less than has been the case, up till now, in Asia. Let us take the example of eroticism.

Shivaism explains the whole cosmos in terms of sexuality: it posits desire at the basis of everything:

> We desire things only insofar as they afford us pleasure. Divinity is an object of love only because it represents an unadulterated delight. . . . The desire of the lustful man for a woman exists only because he sees in her the form of his pleasure, the source of his delight. In the joy of possession, the suffering of desire is momentarily relieved . . . and man perceives in pleasure his own essential nature, which is joy. All joy, all pleasure is an experience of the divine. . . . But perfect love is that love whose object is not limited. It is that love which is pure, the love of love itself, the love of the transcendent Being-of-pleasure.[26]

Kama, the god of erotic pleasure, is worshipped by the yogis "because it is Kama alone, when he is satisfied, who can free the spirit from desire. . . . It is not pleasure but desire that binds man, and that is an obstacle to his spiritual progress." [27] And further: "He who seeks love in the hope of pleasure is the victim of desire. The sage accepts sensual pleasures when they come, but with a detached heart. He is not the victim of desire." [28]

Compare this all-accepting "detachment," this approval of pleasure as the experience of the divine, with the diatribes of a Saint Paul announcing the "wrath of

[26] *Lingopasana Rahasya.*
[27] Alain Daniélou, *Le Polythéisme Hindou*, p. 474.
[28] *Gopala-uttara-tapini Upanishad.*

God, revealed from heaven" against the "shameless" and the "infamous," against "all those who have abandoned themselves to impurity, according to the lusting of their heart." Compare the *Shiva Purāna*, the *Kama Sūtra*, the *Mahābhārata*, the copious commentaries on the phallic cult, with the treatises of the Church Fathers on asceticism and chastity, and it is evident how right Kierkegaard was when he said that Christianity, by condemning sensuality in the name of the spirit, posited it as a reality and a spiritual category.

In the literatures of Asia, there are few convincing examples—I myself know none at all—of what we call love-as-passion, and we know to what degree this form of love depends on its expressions. Passion and mystical love, eroticism and love of one's neighbor are Western *problems* raised for everyone by the ill-endured rigors of dogmas and *imperative* doctrines, while the ways of Asian wisdom are merely *proposed*—and only to some. The recipes for pleasure, or for immortality by the retention of semen, are linked in Asia to piety, while our Western customs derive from an old pagan source and our modern hygiene attempts to be "scientific." Because of the nature of Christianity and of the nature of Hinduism or of Buddhism, actual life in the West is in conflict with faith, while actual life in Asia is in symbiosis with its religions.

And if the symmetry of these formulations is disconcerting, let us turn to examples from everyday life: rather than assembling an infinite bibliography to support my statements, consider this amusing observation from a modern novel, whose author happens to be a Vedantist Brahman: "Living in Europe as I did, and having a French wife, seemed in their eyes to give me some special privilege in the understanding of love." [29]

Further, the cliché of Orient and nonself versus Occident and person, which is perhaps less current in the Orient than in certain American and European circles enraptured by Asiatic wisdom, suggests two remarks, of unequal importance it is true, and deliberately disconcerting.

I. CAUTION IN USING THE DIALECTICAL METHOD. Western man answers the challenge of his sublime dogmas that claim to transfigure concrete life with myths symbolizing his natural resistance and constituting the focus of his erotic life. But the Orient merely proposes "ways" to the Renouncers (or sannyasins) who have drained or who disdain the cup. No drama, still less any tragedy, and above all no all-or-nothing—but countless varieties of approach to the ultimate reality. Where we see contradiction, antinomy, they do not get up on their high theological horses, but each takes his own way, his *svadharma*, his private religion. This is why our Western contradictions remain so fiercely linked to

[29] Raja Rao, *The Serpent and the Rope* (New York, Pantheon Books, 1963), p. 28. I cannot urge my readers strongly enough to read this beautiful autobiographical novel: the poetic freshness or better still the spiritual euphoria which imbues the work situates in reality what I can only formulate here. I know nothing in literature that confronts East and West more tenderly and more rigorously. I also recommend, though it is much less tender, even harsh, to both, Henri Michaux's masterpiece, *A Barbarian in Asia* (New York, New Directions, 1949).

dogma, while their divergences do not oppose each other. If some of their beliefs seem to merge into our own (seem to affirm, for instance, the reality of the person or of the neighbor), we must not assume that such beliefs exclude their contrary, or that we were mistaken as to the true meaning of their repeated affirmations of the contrary (for example, the nonexistence of the self). Let us illustrate this.

The idea of a personal vocation fulfilled at the individual's expense is certainly not hard to find in the Bhagavad-Gītā:

> Be detached and do what is your duty, for in doing his duty without attachment, man achieves the ultimate. (III, 19)
> Our own duty, however humble, is worth more than another's, however successfully accomplished. Another man's *dharma* is full of dangers. (III, 35)

And in the Upanishads:

> Life has served to no purpose for the man who leaves this world without having achieved his own interior world. It remains unlived, like the unrecited Vedas, or any unaccomplished action. (*Brihad-arānyaka*) [30]

The notion of love of one's neighbor, and the evangelical enjoinder to love one's enemy are also to be found in Buddhism: for one's enemy and oneself differ only by the attachments of the phenomenal self, while they participate in the same true Self, which is the only

[30] This passage occurs in the *Brihad-arānyaka*, during the dialogue between the famous legendary sage Yajnavalkya and his bride Maitreyi, who questions him about immortality.

thing that matters. "Surmount evil by good," Buddha says. "May those who calumniate me, harm me, mock me, and all the rest, obtain spiritual illumination," says Shantideva.

And Suzuki, who has taught Zen to so many Americans disgusted with the West, and to a growing number of Europeans as well, goes so far as to say that the Buddhist method "consists in transforming Eros into Agapè." [31]

I repeat, none of this is contradictory in a philosophy without dogmatics. Shall we then speak of a logical inconsistency? But has not our own science invented several logics, each as valid as the next? They contradict each other no more than the spiritual statements corresponding to different levels of development, to different degrees of awakened consciousness.

2. TRIAL BY EXPERIENCE. In Raja Rao's novel mentioned earlier, this sentence from an Upanishad appears several times over:

> *For whose sake, verily, does a husband love his wife?*
> *Not for the sake of his wife, but verily for the sake of*
> *the Self in her.*

Confronted with such a statement, I feel this first of all: the sense of an immediate and lively *recognition*. For all truth about love is immediately recognized by a man in search of knowledge about his love. Anyone

[31] D. T. Suzuki, *Mysticism, Christian and Buddhist*, p. 73. I am afraid the author espouses the categories of *Love in the Western World* rather more than is desirable from his own point of view.

will tell me that the Self of India is not the true God of the Christians, Who is personal. We know the definitions. But here I encounter my own experience. It is only *starting from here* that our questions become capable of being answered. One might write a whole book on this sentence from the Upanishads, on the dialogue that can start from experiences of recognition. (But what if that were the book I am writing? The book which happens to end just here?)

I was saying that true love means to discern in another person—having recognized it in oneself first of all—the true Self, subject of love, and to help it become conscious of what it is or can become. Is this not to help it reflect the light of creative love? No, that would be saying both too much and not enough. To love is to help the other person locate himself in such a way that the light sees *itself* in him, but so that the lover's true Self discovers itself there at the same time, differently illuminated and thereby subtly changed, a little more itself than before: mutual love.

The experience is the same, or at least so I feel it. But the light? Is it the name we give it which is different —or something else? The point of the dialogue is here. Only a point, without extension, but depending on the look we turn upon it, one world or the other is revealed: Western or Eastern.

All the risks of error are on our side; we pay for them by neuroses or spiritual dullness. The Eastern mystics are so much on guard against illusion that they have made it a common factor in everything that exists (the mere fact of existing becomes, for them, the equivalent of our original sin). They have done the same for the neuroses which attack our individual "aggregates": the cosmos as a whole seems to result—according to their sages—from a gigantic schizophrenia of the Self. (But it will ultimately be reabsorbed, everything will come out all right.) They have done the same for the persons potentialized in a single cosmic Person (*Purusha*, whose actualizing counterpart is *Prakriti*), finally dissociated and dissolved in the Self: "You are That." The individual drama is drowned in the Whole. But the Whole is the contrary of the drama.

All the risks of error are linked to our love; and the more passionate, exigent, and singular love is, the greater the risk. Is what we believe we love in *her* herself or the image of our Angel? Is what we think we see in her —and what we may deify at her expense—our projected *anima?* All the psychoanalysts have told us so: error about the person of the beloved is the source of the worse conflicts, a violence done to her soul, to her body, or to her spirit—or even to her total Self, unrecognized, unrespected in its autonomy.

Here the Brahman intervenes:

"If you seek the Self through her, if you have understood impermanence and train yourself to 'true vision' as Buddha said—who was one of us, an Indian—if you see what you are and turn your love to the immutable alone, all these errors you feared are illusory. Like the Self."

I answer:

" 'The true vision' distinguishes and judges, but cannot deny the problem. In this virtually undifferentiated Self that life offers us, with its genetic program unfathomably older than our natural individual, and that will survive it in the course of centuries, without surprises and a thousand times reincarnated—the true vision imagines, in the strongest sense, the person. We must not throw away life with error, but love better. Not extinguish or transcend, but transmute, transfigure! Loving better means learning to distinguish the reason for being—thus for being unique—of the loved Other, as of oneself. This visible body which is animated by a singular and fascinating movement of being. . . . 'Love what you will never see twice over!' "

The Brahman replies:

"Loving is desiring the immortal, not the ephemeral, which has nothing in itself that deserves love. This does not deny the possibility of poetry, of *amours poétiques*, of desire, nor of that adoration woman needs 'for her fulfillment, for in worshipping her we know the world and annihilate it, absorbing it into ourself. We should be Shiva that woman be dissolved—and with her the world. For the world is meant not for denial but for dissolution.' " [32]

I answer:

"I want to see the Other in her reality, which is unique. I love in her both what I see and what makes me see her unique: that True Self anticipated by love

[32] Phrases borrowed like several others in this dialogue from Raja Rao's novel *The Serpent and the Rope*.

alone, and which is *her*self. You say *the* Self, which is
no one."

The Brahman answers:

"There is no one. No one can love except the egoist.
There is love, and we can only become love. And you
know that you must love only your 'God' in His
creatures, since it is said of Him that He is love."

I reply:

"But God, for us, is a Person, and creates us as
distinct persons. You do not *see* the woman you believe
you love."

The Brahman answers:

"When I can love the Self in her, I shall no longer
be me, she will no longer be herself, and the gods themselves will serve me."

ALL AND EACH

The Orient wants to extenuate, "to emaciate the tangible
reality," [33] to rejoin the primordial One. When its gods
themselves shall have done their work and served their
time, there will be the *Self alone in all*.

At the end of time, Saint Paul replies, "*God will be
all in each*."

For the last six thousand years, the sages of Asia
have not varied in their belief in the duality of the One
and the Many, a duality ultimately illusory, since some
day—whose date they know—life, the cosmos, and the

[33] P. Teilhard de Chardin, *La Route de l'Ouest* (unpublished).

gods will be reabsorbed into the single One, without leaving any trace, as though not having taken place. The triumph of these religious thinkers and of their eschatology will be identified, on that day, with the conclusion of an entirely material process calculated by Western science: but no one will be here to bear witness that their doctrines on the final Illumination and the Void will have been, in their totality, only an immense transposition to the poetic and religious planes of the Second Law of Thermodynamics.

The other half of humanity firmly believes in the tangible, insufficient, mysterious reality of actual appearances, which it attempts, in consequence, to examine and modify. It bets on life and against entropy.[34] This half of humanity no longer knows the source of its passion, which has produced technology and science, but also our social structures and politics, the rights of man, and an extraordinary avidity. The real meaning of the adventure escapes the majority of those it sweeps in its course. And it is true that we can scarcely conceive of that adventure without a vision of its anticipated end. The little phrase of Saint Paul at the beginning of the Christian era, "God all in each," in a single flash of light describes that end.

Henceforth: —the duel of the One and the Many is replaced by the drama of the One and the community of unique persons;

[34] It might be fruitful to interpret the Carnot-Clausius principle (the general increase of entropy, luminous death) in terms of *Oriental* metaphysics, and Pauli's principle of exclusion (individuation of electrons, conditioning "life") in terms of *Occidental* metaphysics.

—the final annihilation in unison, by the harmony of an infinite chorus;

—the regressive extinction of ephemeral differences, by their death and transfiguration;

—the individual annihilated in a long aspiration of *Atman*, by the personal eternalized by the vivifying effort of the Imagination.

These are two doctrines, two mystical views. Which is true? If the sages of the Orient are right, no one will be able to verify it at the end of time, not even the Self which will be fast in its dreamless sleep—their notion of happiness—between two totally meaningless Creations. If the Western saints are right, they alone will be there to know it.

The doctrine that can become true will be the one that we choose, truly lived in awareness and action.

The present and historical results are infinitely ambiguous, for our means of measurement. The people of the world are unhappily ignorant of the origins and ends of what they believe, although they live on it more or less well, and even though they sometimes die for their beliefs.

We see what the Orient has remained up till now, and that its doctrines of extinction have not killed the illusion of the self; on the contrary, this valueless self is in the process of imposing its claims, by several hundreds of millions of mouths to feed, and tomorrow of minds to direct. We anticipate in terror and hope what the West can become: either engulfed in the illusion of matter (and the Orient will have been right), or fulfilling its adventurous vocation—to decipher Being in the singular and in the structures of universal energy. For it is by the secret of persons that we try to hear the Person, but it is in matter that we are seeking the Self. "The more we know individual things," Spinoza says, "the more we know God."

All creation, "subject to vanity," yet in "earnest expectation," waits for the "manifestation of the sons of God." (Romans 8.) And Saint Justin the Ecumenical, in the second century, dared speak of a salvation of matter. By grasping it in his hands, measuring it with his eyes, dissolving and recomposing it, spying like the alchemist on the secret life of this matter of the expanding cosmos, of the elusive atom, of the living body, Western man seeks not only to discover its secret laws, but to transform himself, insofar as he participates in the mystery of creation. He has chosen this way; let him follow it to its end! For him, Reality is in the individual, and Being in the *raison d'être* of the unique person. His choice is that of love, of knowledge by love, for everything that exists is unique when seen close to, as love sees.

BETWEEN THE VOID AND
THE KINGDOM

THAT ALL the matter of the cosmos, gathered together, could be contained in a die; that on this little earth hanging in the Void, we walk upon the Void and toward the Void, being ourselves but furtive aggregates of dusty statistical clouds; that according to science and its truth all is void in the dimensions of the universe (millions of light-years in space, billions of terrestrial years in time), and that at the bottom of calculable reality is the Void—but that, twinklings in the history of this seed, our earth, past civilizations seem great and majestic to us; further, that at the turn of a path followed in the April woods a revelation of pure happiness awaits us; that the inflection of a voice is enough for an encounter, tomorrow, to be the point of our life; that there are such moments when we are convinced that "everything" depends on a decision to be made; that a colorful, accessible, dense, and stable world spreads around us as we proceed into its duration: that there is, then, all this but the Void, all this *in* the Void and composed of the Void, steeped and impregnated with vacuity, this dizzying awareness silently accompanies the thoughts of men today, and their action.

The miracle is that there are forms! That there are consistency, landscapes, faces, a Nature around us that henceforth seems grace and gift: miraculous; and that vacuity could have given birth to the plenitude of bodies, that light should have become vision, energy emotion, structure myth, and gravitation desire.

What first troubles and ultimately scandalizes the mind of the Oriental mystic is precisely what constitutes my joy—the transformation of the cloud of billions of divisible aggregates into the desire for an animate body, for a unique form liberated from that colorless transparency which is the primal curse, the cosmic hell.

Incarnation is our grace. It alone creates color, touch, distance, and music, the lithe resilience of the flesh and the desire that will not halt in its pursuit of a transcendent plenitude, the Pleroma.

For this Nature, which seems miraculous, is still only a mirage reflected upon the Void, if it is not a parable of the Eternal. These forms remain allusive, these bodies suffer and die, these feelings err, this desire demands an Elsewhere in which possession is complete.

Of course science now gives us one "elsewhere" or another whose mere possibility the last centuries thought they had banished: it calculates them precisely. What are they for our desire? This Void that bathes everything? Antimatter? Other parallel worlds that would be the negative of our own? But we want a Beyond, and not the opposite of our agonies and our joys, a Beyond that transforms, and not a reflection!

A minor and perfect poet of our time discovered it one day, not without amazement:

"There is another world, but it is in this one." [1]

[1] Paul Eluard.

What did he mean? What had he seen? What other world? And why should there be only one?

There is the world of the Void, the other world of science: it is here, among us, here and now, and we do not see it, although assured of its imminent presence. It is not ourselves.

But there is *within us* the Kingdom! The Kingdom "which is not of this world," and which is yet "within us," for it is more ourselves than we are, since it is in each of those who receive it as "the Son of God," the celestial share, the warrant of the Angel that will be "our effigy" in the circle of fire that Dante saw. And by what parable shall we represent it? "It is like a grain of mustard seed, which, when it is sown in the earth, is less than all the seeds that be in the earth: But when it is sown, it groweth up . . . and shooteth out great branches; so that the fowls of the air [*the angels*] may lodge under the shadow of it." [2] It is not in space and time, which extend the Void to the dimensions of the universe; it is not *far* from here or from now, from the world of forms, which is Nature, the Parable—but here and now, and in thyself. The Kingdom of Heaven is a point, the point of eternity posited within you, the seed of the Pleroma to come, when "the image of this world shall pass away" and the invisible shall be seen. When you know it, then love begins, and love has already begun, for it is love that knows it within you.

If thought finds no answer to the fundamental question asked by the Void: *Why not nothing?* it surrenders

[2] Mark 4:31-32.

233

to the Void and is reduced to nothing. What can retain it on the brink of nothing is the direct intuition of love.

It is because of love that there is something, that the Void is animated, differentiated, that there are forces which attract and repel each other, and therefore compose each other; that there is form and movement, near and far in space and time, world and person, desire, suffering and joy. And we can love these forms because love has formed them: we recognize it in them, as it calls them into being in us.

Love alone explains everything, and being-in-itself is only a word designating the inconceivable: what would exist without love, "that which is" *minus* love by which alone there is something. Love alone, therefore, can say: I am. Without love, there would not even be the Void. Love has created the Void by displaying the attraction which is called energy in the physical, desire in the animic order. And this alone gives a meaning to everything: to the cosmic void in which this or that fog of random electrons dance and which suddenly can say *I*, can say *you* when it sees the self in the other, can say: *I am;* but also at that turn of the path in the April woods, a tiny, complex, and fortuitous world, earth and stones, wet grass, bright sky between the hawthorn branches, here, nowhere, and why did I love it? *Why not nothing?* Because that turn in the path made me a sign and was at that moment a sign for me, existing in my recognition, and because every sign or sense manifests love; and nothing else really matters: nothing else in the world summons me.

I might have doubted being, and becoming, and all our ideas about "God": I have never doubted love itself. I might have doubted almost all the truths of Western morality and culture—before recovering several of them, better understood, upon my return from an Orient of the mind. I have doubted most of the truths successively demonstrated by our sciences; and I do not cease to doubt our image of the world, the Void, and the inconceivable distances calculated starting from our forms. (I anticipate too many short cuts, which will be found!) But I believe I have never doubted all this except by virtue and in the name of love. It is the indubitable grace. I have no *other* certain faith, no other hope, and I see no meaning save love, nor other reasons to doubt, I mean: to seek till the end for what we can someday love with all our being finally realized, in the Whole finally contemplated. When love will be all in each, upon the renewal of all things.

ABOUT THE AUTHOR

BORN in Switzerland in 1906, DENIS DE ROUGEMONT has participated in many of this century's most important intellectual movements. Presently Director of the Centre Européen de la Culture in Geneva, de Rougemont directed French broadcasts over the Voice of America during the war and has been in the forefront of the postwar interest in European unification. He has helped found an impressive number of European cultural organizations and since 1951 has been President of the Executive Committee of the Congress for Cultural Freedom.

De Rougemont, however, is primarily known in the United States for his influential works, *Love in the Western World* and *The Devil's Share*. He is the author of a great many other books, articles and pamphlets, covering the fields of politics, philosophy, theology and literature, which have been translated into twelve languages. *Love Declared* is the sixth of his books to appear in English.